FINDING HER

by
Brittany Weird

ISBN 978-1-0878-5747-3

Cover Design by Mandy Morreale
Cover photography by Thomas Garnett: G-Lens Creative, LLC

IVisionPress.com

To my younger self.

I see you.

You are not alone anymore.

This one is for YOU!

TABLE OF CONTENTS

One
Start Today

Deep down inside we all want to be better people. We all want to break the bad habits and destructive patterns that ruin our lives. We all want to get rid of all that anger and stress to find peace and genuine happiness.

But where do we even start?

That's the famous question I'm sure everyone has found themselves asking at least once in their life. Looking straight in the eyes of a situation or circumstance, and wondering why it happened and what to do now? It's the question I've personally wrestled with for years but was too intimidated to face. It's a question that can literally rob you of your purpose and growth, restrain and delay your future, and ultimately hold you back from all that God has for you.

And because we don't know the answer, we may decide not to start at all.

Why is that? What is holding us back, even though we are unhappy with where we are now?

Well, for me, the answer was fear.

That's right, FEAR!

Fear of the unknown. Fear of the 'what if's.'

Fear of making the wrong decision.

Fear of regret.

Fear of the opinions of others.

Fear of letting someone down, or simply the Fear of never being enough.

And that list goes on and on, with so many Fears holding me back, keeping me from moving forward.

Keeping me from being the woman I want to be.

But today I encourage you, just like I am encouraging myself right now, to JUST START!

If you want to escape all the disasters in your life, if you want to free yourself from Fear, if you want to be better, live better, love more deeply, then just start.

Start somewhere. Start anywhere.

Just start.

Make a decision that, right this minute, you are ready to confront your Fears and start making changes today.

Decide that you are going to stop blaming others and take hold of your own life.

From this point on, you are going to work hard to be the person you always hoped you would be. Someone you can be proud of, deep down inside. Someone who may mess it up a time or two, but then picks herself up, dusts herself off, and keeps moving forward.

And I wrote this book to help you do just that.

I'm not saying it's going to be easy. I may even be convinced it will be the hardest thing you have done in years. But in the end, you'll be happier, and so will those around you.

What you are going to quickly realize is that change can be hard. Really hard. You spent years building up all your defense mechanisms, bad habits, and embarrassing secrets, and they're not going down without a fight. You're going to have to do it terrified and nervous. But if I can go ahead and give you the heads up, then you will hopefully not jump ship and just understand it's a part of the process.

When I finally made the decision to grab the pen and notebook and to share some of my story for the first time, I was terrified too. I didn't know where or how to start. And I almost gave up yet again. The questions flooded my mind and my heart, and it was almost too overwhelming to even think about doing.

But then I realized that there was only one person holding me back from everything that I was supposed to be. And that was me.

No one was hiding the pens and paper from me. No one was grabbing my wrists to stop me from writing. I was literally standing in my own way; self-sabotaging my future because of the lies I was letting myself believe. Lies built up and reinforced by all the bad times and hard things I've been through. Lies that had me believing that authentically sharing my story for the first time would be wrong, because of the others who were tied to it. Lies that told me it would be easier to just keep lying to myself and everyone else, than to tell the truth in this book.

Year after year, I created and built a secret system that devalued my self-worth and disqualified me before I even started. Brick after brick, I built walls inside my soul that kept me from all the opportunities that God had created for me. But I couldn't see it for myself. I had built the walls too high. I had made the system too strong to believe change was possible.

I slowly realized I had this wall up that kept everyone at a distance, including myself, which I've come to realize was only because I didn't know who I was.

Then one day, I decided I had enough of Fear. I decided it was time to let go of everything holding me back and start taking steps in the direction I wanted my life to go. I had hit my version of rock bottom.

And yeah, I know that can be hard in itself, especially when you don't even know what it is you really want for yourself, let alone who you really are deep inside.

That's where you have to start the process of self-discovery. You have to make a conscious decision to be intentional in getting to know yourself, and be willing to work through things, to heal, to forgive, to grow in all areas of your life, because they run hand and hand!

That is where we have to dig, and that's why I am sitting here with you today. Because we are worth it!

Let me say that again…

WE ARE WORTH IT!

You deserve to live your best life, to be genuinely happy, to walk in purpose, to be loved and to love!

Can you accept that fact after all the mistakes you've made, the bad decisions, and the regrets you have? Just remember that, no matter what you've done, those things are in the past, and self-improvement is all about your future.

So start today, with this book, with my encouragement, to accept that you are worthy of a new life, a better attitude, and the many years of happiness that lie ahead.

This is where I want to ask if you want the good news, or the bad news first?

Well, I'm one that always prefers to get bad news out of the way first, so here it goes.

Unfortunately, no mental, physical or emotional growth can happen for you just by coincidence. No one accidentally becomes the best version of their self. It takes work, discipline and even tears. There is a good chance it will cost you relationships that may be holding you back.

After years of building walls to protect your feelings, it will hurt like hell to knock them down. You will feel alone at times. You will have to walk back through some traumatic memories, but don't let that stop you.

The good news is that the person you become on the other side of all that will be worth every second! The peace and clarity you will gain, the appreciation for what you have been able to push through, and the confidence you will have just by surviving will be worth every tear and heartache. And knowing that you are becoming the best version of you is priceless.

I felt led for a long time to inspire, motivate, and push others to find the courage to be their best selves; mentally, emotionally, physically and spiritually. To motivate others to want and expect more for themselves, despite what they have been through or going through, and to do it all unbothered and authentically. That is why I decided to write this book.

But now, I realize this book will be a huge part of my own healing process as well. Telling my story and seeing how I was hurting myself and those around me, made me realize how much I really needed to change. Walking back through all that pain only brought to the surface how much pain I was also causing others. In the same way, Self-reflection and asking the hard questions will have you in the hot seat too.

By recognizing and admitting my mistakes, I took the first steps in letting go of my Fears and regret.

It is my heart's desire that this book helps bring healing to the areas of your life that you may be struggling to find the answers to, or just not fully understanding the *whys* in your life:

Why did all those bad things happen to me?
Why did people treat me like that?
Why did I make the choices I made?
Why am I going through all this now?

That list can go on and on, as well.

Those *why's* without revelation or acceptance can arrest your spirit and have you living beneath your full potential. I pray it pushes you to begin your own journey of self-discovery.

So, if you are ready to put in the work, let's do it!

If you are ready to start, let's go! Remember we are doing this together. I am right there with you.

We got this!!

Two
Some Background

To start off, I want to cover some groundwork, since we are going to be getting pretty up-close and personal throughout this process. I plan on being fully transparent with you. I have to be, for my benefit and yours!

Remember, this is an ongoing process of growth, not a one-day jump to happiness.

In order to get to where I need to be, I have to learn to be real with myself. To let go of all those self-criticisms and regrets holding me back. To move past them and accept the parts of my story that I did not expect to happen the way they did and all those things I cannot control.

With all that, I do not want you to think of this book as a sad story or my personal pity party. It's not. This book is a celebration of growth, my growth. It is written in victory, even if I may not fully see it at this very moment. This book is neither a confessional, nor a gossip session.

That's why I do not have anything negative to say about anyone that is mentioned throughout my story. I am intentional on how I share my truth, without anyone having to play the villain in my story.

I believe in seeing myself as a victor, not a victim.

I've come to a realization that everyone has known hard times and personal pain. Everyone has difficult things that they have been through, and those dents and bruises have shaped them into the people they are today. All those quiet problems that we may never know are why they end up doing what they do, to themselves and others. Whether that be in ways that positively or negatively shaped parts of my life.

The truth is, we are all a little broken, some of us more than others, and whether we realize it or not, we take that brokenness out on the people around us. Hurting them before they can hurt us, or simply because they love us. We toss damage around like candy on Christmas, sometimes not even noticing who it hits. And that can make everyone else a little more broken too.

If you can learn to see past the actions or offenses that people throw at you, it's easier not to take things so personally. If you can accept that something in that person snapping at you has more to do with their internal war than it does with you... When you can understand that something in them is broken too, it gives you the strength to extend grace and the space necessary to heal and forgive.

If there was a villain in this story, I'd say it would have to be me. The 'old me.' The me that spent almost every day punishing herself with fear and regret. The me that didn't love herself correctly. The me that refused to heal. The me that didn't take time to get to know herself. The me that tolerated pain and walked around defeated and broken. The me that didn't take responsibility and own her part in everything I complained about. The me that coddled dysfunction. I see that person – that old me – as the only villain here, which would imply that the 'New Me' is the real hero of the story.

And you can make the New You that you are becoming the hero of your own story too, but only if you are willing to stop the blame game and own all your problems, and if you can take responsibility for the difficult part you must play in this process.

God pressed on my heart that this book needed to be a vital step in my healing process, a necessity for me to reach the next level. My growth is tied to this obedience. Sharing my story, authentically and for the first time, will bring a part of the healing process that can help me move forward whole.

Healing can be such a tricky word and can be used in so many ways and in so many different circumstances that it can feel at times unobtainable in ours. I described healing as a process because that is exactly what it is. If we see healing as some kind of destination, where we suddenly wake up one day and everything is perfect, it can seem overwhelming. The idea of healing can feel so far out of reach that we sit stagnant, not knowing where to even start. But if we think of healing as a process, we only have to take that first step out of our comfort zone to start the journey. As long as we are pointed in the right direction, as long as we are committed to taking action, we can take this journey to our new and better self one day at a time and still feel we are making progress.

As I share some of my story on these pages, I also want to share some of the things that have worked for me. Please keep in mind that we are all different. We all have different upbringings and stories that make us unique. What has worked for me may not work for you and that's okay. Don't let that discourage you. Take all of the suggestions I offer in this book and focus on the ones that work for you.

All I can do is encourage you to dig deep, and to figure out what does work for you, because I can promise you God has so much more waiting for you than where you are at right now!

I know you've been through a lot, but keep this in mind…

Everything you've gone through has served a purpose in your life, if only to identify the things that cause you the most heartache.

And just like your body uses pain to show areas that have been damaged, your soul uses heartache to let you know the areas you most need to work on, in order for you to heal.

I know that right now that may be so hard to hear or fully fathom. I honestly hope you don't shut my book right here and walk away, because believe me when I say I have heard that too many times to count. Every time someone told me that all the bad things I was going through had a purpose, it would make me angry. The idea that my pain and heartache were supposed to have a good side, even during the most devastating times of my life, would literally piss me off. I know, that doesn't even feel right to say. But now, looking back on many of my darkest days, I can see where that pain taught me some valuable life lessons. It created in me the strength I needed to be there for someone else. That pain was a vital resource for this next season of my life. Either way, I've learned that perspective is key.

How we view situations and circumstances can either set us up for a better future or set us up for failure. I've learned this past year especially that our mindset and our thoughts control the direction of our lives. What we allow to play in our heads over and over mentally ends up ruling us. What we allow ourselves to meditate on will only keep cycling through our minds, more and more. What we allow ourselves to meditate on will have us living a life that feels out of control if we don't manage it.

I hate that I was a victim of my own self-destructive thoughts for so long. I was stuck mentally, prisoner to the same thoughts running around crazily in my head, and I honestly thought that was just the way I was.

When operating out of a regret-centered mindset, we let our worst emotions take the driver's seat. All those doubts and hurt thoughts have a tendency to lead us down dead ends, smashing us into walls any chance they get.

Feelings can definitely be overwhelming, but they are also a huge indicator that something within us needs attention.

And just like anything else in life, if we ignore the check engine lights, we will eventually break down.

When I accepted that I had to change my way of thinking, one of the first things I realized is that I couldn't heal in the environment that was hurting me. You can't heal trauma while it's happening. That would be like going to the hospital with a knife in your side and the doctor trying to treat around the knife without ever taking it out. As long as the cause of your pain is still inside you, there's no way to repair the wounds and put you back together again so you can heal.

Every time you moved, that knife in your side would open up the cut and do more internal damage. It would be almost impossible to ignore. Every time you saw the blade, it would remind you of who it was that hurt you and how much pain they caused. It would limit your reach and cause you to splash blood on others. The deeper the wound, the longer that knife stays inside you, the harder it will be to yank it out. But why wouldn't you want to heal, instead of choosing a life of continual pain?

As for me, my knife was buried deep. But I knew that living with so much pain was killing me slowly.

To finally pull the knife out, I had to walk away from a fifteen-year marriage in which we shared two kids, a ministry, and a life that was all I've ever known.

And so, for the first time in my life, I had to make a decision where I had to choose ME and what was best for me at the time.

Three

A Tough Decision

I know what you may be thinking,

"Girl, are you serious? Like you didn't think about how leaving your marriage would affect your kids, your family, and the people that look up to y'all?"

But not all relationships are healthy. Not all marriages are made in heaven.

How many people marry someone without even asking God if they should?

Just think of how many divorces there are these days, how many women end up in therapy, in shelters…or worse.

And sometimes, caring for your own mental and emotional health makes the people in your life healthier as well. It can be the right thing to do, best for everyone involved, even if it may look like selfishness to others. Otherwise, you risk spreading your fears and brokenness to those you love. Making more and more people miserable as you try as hard as you can, day after day, to swallow your pain.

I had done enough spreading my own pain to others, making them partners in my brokenness. Even if it seemed selfish to everyone on the outside, I realized it was the kindest thing I could do for my children.

So that's what I did. I thought about all of that and realized something…

How can I be what everyone else needs when I can't be what I need for myself? How can I love others when I'm not even loving myself?

I was in a place where I felt I was slowly suffocating, barely breathing, just going through the motions, living on auto pilot. I was constantly on edge, reacting instead of responding in most situations. Now I realize that is what led to so many fogged memories.

Have you ever had someone ask you about a time that you should remember…but you don't? I've heard that the way the brain protects us from long term trauma. When you mentally check out, for whatever reason, your brain cannot store memories. It's like hitting a pause, instead of recording. That's where I was in life. I was there, but not there.

Alive, but not living.

I remember getting to such a low place within myself, that I knew there could be no way this is how God meant for me to live.

Still, it was by far the hardest decision I have ever had to make. So much was at stake if I was wrong.

Of course, there were many variables that led up to my deciding it was best for the both of us if I leave. But in the end, it was what needed to happen for us to get better individually. Still, I felt like I was hanging on the edge of the cliff, and from where I was standing, it was a long, long way down.

In the beginning we were just kids looking into this new adventure we were about to embark on. We were feeling excited for whatever came our way because we had each other. I had him and he had me. I felt like I had won a prize because he chose me above everyone else. I loved being around him. He made me laugh and gave my life purpose.

I found happiness in just making him happy. I loved to surprise him and make him feel loved. For example, I threw him some epic birthday parties. One of my favorites had a Fear Factor theme. He was just turning twenty-five, and Fear Factor was a real popular show at that time. We always had fun watching it together.

Like the show, I had some strange, and somewhat disgusting challenges. A few brave friends of ours even ate crickets! It was hard to believe. But the party was a blast, and we laughed until we cried. To see him smile made me smile. We loved cookouts and we made a great team at cornhole games. We won a lot of tournaments together. We were both very competitive. We even had a ping pong table in our living room and would often play right up until bedtime.

But, like most things, laughter fades and those very few memories of good times are not always enough to hold a failing marriage together.

If you are wondering, no, I didn't have a plan. I had no idea what I was going to do, or what it was going to look like, or how I was going to make it. If I'm being honest, I was terrified. When you're in the middle of such a life-changing decision, it's easy to doubt yourself and everything you were so sure of even the day before.

But I made the decision that I knew was best for me and would be best for my family. Period. I had to fully trust that God would do His part if I trusted His voice and did mine. As difficult as it was, I had to stay confident in knowing He had a plan for me, even with all my pain and uncertainty.

For all the holier-than-thou religious people that may be reading this from a judgmental angle, wondering "How can you say God led you to get a divorce?"

It is a good question, and one I struggled with at the time, and even now, still do. But way too many people pass judgement before knowing all the details, without understanding what it feels like to watch everything you are, and everything you have slip away, piece by piece. It's so easy to condemn someone who's life is falling apart, if you've never experienced that yourself.

For people who'd rather criticize than sympathize, my response is that from that perspective the details will never matter, because of the lens they are choosing to view it from will always be negative. Just as we too often focus on our own faults, some people only choose to see the faults and failings of others.

Judgement separates us. Love and understanding bring us together.

But to better help the ones with a sincere heart who are wondering what led to my decision…well, there's a lot that played a part in that. I didn't just wake up one day and say, "Ya know what? I don't want to do this anymore."

I never planned on getting a divorce. I mean, does anyone? I fought for a very long time with everything in me to make my marriage work. Honestly! That's why I can be at peace with my decision to leave, because I know at the end of the day I gave it my all for a very long time. And up until that point, I really didn't believe divorce was an option. I mean, we do vow for better or worse, in sickness and in health, but it wasn't “Biblical” to just get a divorce because it was hard at times.

You can keep dealing with things and pray they get better. But when you feel there is no way out, that you are growing numb to life and just counting the days until you die, you know something is seriously wrong. Like I said, it was a fifteen-year marriage, that's a long time, half my life! A lot can and did happen in that length of time, but one thing I know that was evident was that I married too young. I said my vows when I was only fifteen years old.

Looking back, especially now that I have a daughter who just turned fifteen, I'm like, yeah, right, AIN'T NO WAY!!

She's still a child, a kid that is still growing, developing becoming and learning who she is. She is way too young to understand what she would be getting into. Too young to make a decision about the rest of her life. Too young to know who would be right for her.

I'm not going to say that getting married at fifteen wasn't the best thing for me at that time, because in so many ways, it was! My marriage saved my life! I know what you may be thinking, how, right!?

Four

My Marriage

Growing up, I hadn't always made the best decisions.

I was raised without a lot of guidance and ended up getting myself into a lot of trouble at a very young age. I thought I had it all figured out. At fifteen, I was abusing drugs and already had a few run-ins with the police. But the one that took the cake was when I got caught selling drugs in middle school. That's right. Even though I was a kid myself, I was committing a felony by selling drugs to other kids who were fourteen years old or younger

So much for having everything figured out.

The police came to my school to arrest me. I remember sitting in the principal's office for what felt like hours while the discussed a decision that could change the trajectory of my life. As a kid, it's so easy to make decisions sometimes, never knowing what consequences they will bring, or the impact they will have on your future. When I asked to use the bathroom, a female officer handcuffed me and walked me through the halls of my own school. I tried my best to act tough, because that's what I thought you had to do. There I was, escorted to the bathroom in handcuffs like a criminal, but in their defense, which I guess was true. Imagine the shame I felt, hoping all my peers couldn't see how terrified I really was. The eyes of my fellow students felt like a million spotlights exposing a weak little girl hiding under this fragile shell.

The hall I used to walk with my head held high was now a hall I slunk down with my tail between my legs. Once we got to the bathroom, I had to leave the door open to make sure I wasn't trying to flush any evidence down the toilet. Being watched in the bathroom, I felt violated and embarrassed. When it was time to get my mother on the phone and inform her what was going on, I held my breath. The second I heard her say 'hello,' a tear dropped from my eye. I knew how much I was about to disappoint her. Regardless of everything she had allowed me to do, deep down a mother still wants what's best for her child, even though my mom was never taught how to help me achieve that.

She cried and I cried, and we said our "I love you's" before hanging up. Then I was placed in the back of a police car for my one-hour drive to the Hardin County Juvenile Detention Center. The whole way, I went through all the possibilities of what I was about to walk into. I was scared and just wanted to go home; I wanted my mom. I had no idea what to expect but I knew it wouldn't be good. I started to think about my siblings and how my actions would affect them.

I was arrested on a Friday, so I knew I was going to be in there for at least a couple days because of the weekend. When I arrived, I went through the process of getting checked in. They stripped me down and searched me and I was placed in a holding cell for the first twenty-four hours. There I was…alone, no tv, no window, just me, a lot of metal objects and a million thoughts running through my head of how in the world I got here. I had a few piercings at the time, and they made me take them out so I could not use them to hurt myself or other people. I remember twisting off the skinny pieces of my comb, and every so often, sticking them through the holes to make sure they didn't close up. Priorities, right?

Breakfast was early. Like ridiculously early for a teen. I think it was like 5 AM. They didn't do a regular wake-up call; more like a wake-up bang. Loud yelling and metal-on-metal clanging were the first sounds I heard as I awoke to my first day in general population. It was a tough adjustment to have people dictate every second of your day, with no freedom at all. They tell you what to do and when to do it.

I will say I was expecting to have issues with some girls in there. I was mentally prepared for conflict, but everyone was really nice and welcoming. I was very grateful for that because I feel that would have made my experience worse than what it already was. We shared our stories and lives outside of these walls, and what we planned to do when we got out. Some were serving months, some days. I was unsure of what my future looked like because I wouldn't know until my court date when I would receive my sentencing.

I remember one night in particular. There was a girl that had a beautiful voice. She would sing at night, and it was so peaceful. It helped remind me that there can be moments in life where, despite where we are at, we get a brief glimpse of a lily in the valley. I'd like to think that God had her there just for me; to remind me there can be beauty in even the ugliest situations. I didn't realize it then, but I see that now. God's work all around us.

After five days in jail, I was released. My mom and grandma picked me up and I couldn't wait to get home and back to 'my normal.' We stopped and got "real" food and I lit a cigarette almost immediately. Old habits die hard, I guess. That night I was out on my back porch with the fam, passing a joint around and telling them all about my experience in juvie.

In the end, I was sentenced to sixty hours of community service, and put in an alternative school with other kids who had also made bad decisions or were slipping out of control. Even though I knew what I had done to get there, I felt I didn't belong in that place, and ended up dropping out of school in the eighth grade.

So, there I was...a fourteen-year-old with a drug problem and criminal record, who had been kicked out of school. I didn't have much hope things would ever get better.

That is, until I met the man who would soon become my husband.

My sentence involved doing community service at the same alternative school I was forced to attend. I was actually doing my hours after school, where they also held GED classes. That's why he was there. I was tired and had stayed up most of the night before. Not only that, when I was released from juvie I slowly fell back into my normal habits, so I had taken some pretty heavy drugs. I had on baggy sweats with handprints on the butt with one leg rolled up. Yeah, just one. I guess I thought I was a G. I was carrying some chairs from one building to the next and dropped one, when this good-looking man offered to help. Then he asked if I had a lighter for his cigarette. I didn't, but that carried into some small talk. We flirted and then he asked me for my number. He was older than me, seemed nice and like I said, I thought he was really cute. His style was that baggy pants and shirt, some Jordans. Swaggy. Just my type.

We started talking on the phone at night and hit it off really quickly. When he asked how old I was, I told him I was sixteen, which was a lie. I was scared if he knew the truth, he wouldn't even give me a chance. I feel I was mature for my age considering I ran around a lot with my older brother and had dated some of his friends. When the truth came out, he was upset but admitted he had already started to fall for me, so it didn't matter. I was so relieved. We were with each other a lot in the beginning, and I just loved being around him. He made me happy.

My future husband was eighteen when we met and seemed to be the opposite of everything I was used to. For the first time, I saw a completely different side to life. One that seemed stable and had more to it than just the next high or wild party. All that seemed both scary and welcoming to me.

He grew up in church, something I knew about but never had really been introduced to before. My mom would say our prayers at night when she tucked us in, you know the "Now I lay me down to sleep, I pray the lord my soul to keep," but that was really the extent of it. My grandparents were in church, and we went with them a few times but nothing regular. But this was different. This man really believed. Through him, I ended up being introduced to God – not a vengeful God who condemned me for the things I had done, but a loving Father who wanted the best for me, even when I had failed. This was something new for me – unconditional love.

Up until that point, I can't recall really "loving" anyone, other than my family, and some of them even missed the mark on what I now define as love. But this man was different. He was passionate for God when we met. We quit smoking together, and he even encouraged me to be mindful of how I dressed and the music I listened to. I remember getting into his car and trying to turn it onto a hip hop station, and he would change it to something like Gospel Gangsters, a rap group he listened to at the time. He was the real deal. He loved my siblings and just seemed like an all-around perfect guy, and let's not forget he was fine. I was open to hearing him out because it was the first time in my life that I had ever felt like someone had my best interest at heart. He took me to church and even had the conversation about not wanting to have sex before marriage, even though neither of us were virgins. And when we did mess up, he felt and expressed conviction. He had a big heart and was helping raise his nephew and cousin. Very active in both of their lives as the only male figure. His cousin actually came with us on our first official date. He asked if I would mind if he tagged along and of course I said no. We went to the fair and had a great time. He won me this huge bear from this basketball game. It was as big as me, and we had to carry that thing around the whole time.

I admired everything about him. He had an amazing family who loved me like their own. Even with everything I had done, and everything I continued to struggle with, I felt accepted by the church, by his family, and by a God who cared deeply about me.

And so, I fell in love with God, at the same time, falling in love with the guy that introduced me to Him. I say 'love,' but really, they were two different kinds of love. My feelings for my future husband had a lot of lust involved, as well. I guess had no idea what real love really was.

Something else I recognized, and this one took a while to accept, was that I had become overly attached to him very early on in an unhealthy way. It's embarrassing to admit, but I did promise you complete transparency.

Children are sponges. We learn how to love from what we see in our homes growing up. We use our parents as a model for our own future relationships and how to deal with our own children as they grow. We can either copy their success, or we find that one day, we are doomed to repeat their mistakes. In our early childhood years, we learn to either develop a sense of our own value…or end up seeing ourselves as not worth loving at all.

Unfortunately, not everyone gets the storybook childhood. Not all of us grow up in the kind of loving and supportive home you see on television. I'm sure my parents struggled to do their best, as most parents do, but when I was young, I never saw love properly displayed from either parent. Home was where you started out, until you were brave enough to run away from it.

Now, as an adult, I feel growing up like this taught me everything I didn't want to be and everything not to do to my own children.

I had come from a broken home. My father was never around when I was growing up, and I missed having a strong male figure in my life. Who knows whether I would have made the same mistakes if I had a caring dad around for guidance…one who could show me my worth? Or if my mother would have known how to constructively discipline me, or teach me never to settle and how much I had to offer? Or even parents who loved each other and demonstrated what a healthy relationship could be?

My mom and dad were never married and honestly, were not even together that long. I guess you could say I was an accident or a surprise. Thankfully, my mom still chose to keep me. She already had two other kids by different fathers, none of whom were present or helped financially. Despite that, we never went without anything we needed, and I always felt mom found a way, no matter what she had to do. Mom did struggle with some substance abuse, and we were taken by Child Protective Services due to an abandonment charge which was only partially true. I was like six years old. The story was that she had left us with her friend while she went out-of-state to score some marijuana. According to her, she ended up having car problems, and what was supposed to be a weekend ended up being much longer. She said that back then, it was harder to communicate, so she was unable to let the friend she had caring for us know what was going on. So, after a while, she was turned in for abandonment. CPS looked into the issue and felt it was in our best interest to remove us from our home for a period of time. My mom fought like hell and did everything she could to get us back, and eventually she did. There's not one ounce of me that feels my mom wouldn't do anything in this world for me if she could, but sometimes she just doesn't know how.

Growing up my mom was a fighter and did whatever was necessary to make a way. One thing I loved while growing up was how she always cooked dinner, and for the most part, we ate at the table as a family. Being a single mom, she shut the kitchen down at a certain time, she would say, "The kitchen is closed," which meant stay out in a nice way. She would then hustle us off to our baths, before tucking us in at night. I'm sure she needed some time for herself and getting us in bed gave her some alone time. Looking back, I see the lack of love she received as a child, and the daddy issues she struggled with her whole life shaped a lot of why she did what she did. The excessively disciplined little girl inside her came to look at discipline in a negative way, so she didn't know how to set and enforce rules without it triggering some very painful memories. She found that simply coping was easier than feeling.

Over the years, I came to empathize with her and not hold her hostage to her actions, which were influenced by a lack of knowledge and all she went through personally. That's not an entirely free pass. My mom's own choices made her life a little harder. We were forced to move a lot, and for a period of time, all of us shared a single bedroom at my grandparents' house. Luckily, it was a king-size bed.

I watched her work hard to always make sure we never went without the necessities. We didn't get to go on vacations or have extravagant birthdays, but we had what we needed and that was enough. She looked for love in men and when it no longer was there, she moved on. She ended up having two other kids by another man. That meant five kids from four different fathers. The last of those fathers was named Greg, and he actually took on some of the father roles that I lacked. I remember him helping me with homework and just being the most present, until that ended pretty traumatically. He was arrested for assault on my mother.

This shocked me because I saw Greg as the gentlest giant ever. He stood six-foot, four-inches tall and always seemed so kind. I never remember him even raising his voice. Greg usually never drank, but one night, he came home really intoxicated. He and mom got into it and all I remember is a lot of yelling and screaming, and then seeing blood everywhere. I'm not sure if I called the cops, but I feel I did. I was young, probably like nine or ten. I was terrified and torn. Every part of me wanted to hug Greg, because I saw regret in his eyes and knew he didn't mean to hurt my mom, but the other side felt terrible for my mom, seeing how beat up she was. When the police showed up, they took one look at my mom's face and slammed Greg to the ground even though he wasn't resisting. They treated him like an animal, and it broke my heart. To my young mind, I felt sorry for him and my mom at the same time. I didn't know who was right or wrong, I just wished it hadn't happened. After they took

Greg away, Mom shuffled us back to our grandparents' one bedroom, only now with two more babies to fit in the bed. Again, I thank God for that king-size bed!

Mom had only been married twice. One marriage was with my older brother's dad before I was born so I don't remember that one, but the second time shocked us all. She went away with a guy she was dating and came home married. No formal ceremony for us to be a part of. No warning at all, just a "we're married" when she finally got home. That relationship lasted a little longer than the others but would end in a traumatic experience as well.

I was twelve years old when I heard a loud noise in the kitchen and ran downstairs. There was my latest stepdad bleeding from his head and my mom yelling. She had thrown a glass plate at him, which left him a big gash across his forehead. I stood there frozen, not knowing what to do. The cops were on their way and mom was telling us kids to tell the cops that he threw the glass plate at her and she was just trying to block it when it came back and hit him in the head. That's a lot of pressure to put on kids. Well, her story didn't hold up and they took my mom in. She was released pretty quickly and started figuring out what was next for us, now that the latest stepdad was out of the picture. We were left alone a lot. Which left room for things to happen at early ages that shouldn't. One of my sisters was five years older than me, and I watched her sneak boys in after mom left for work at nights. She even introduced me to things I had no business knowing at that time. When Mom found out about the boys, she took a baseball bat to my sister's room, wrecking everything! My older sister had already stayed a lot with my grandparents, but after the destruction of her room, she ended up moving in with them. That would actually work out for the best because she had diabetes that was very hard to keep regulated. She was in and out of the hospital all the time, and it was hard for my mom to keep jobs when she would have to miss work because my sister was sick.

As I got older, I was introduced to a lifestyle of drugs and alcohol from everyone in my life. My dad was an alcoholic and that's what has kept him from being present in my life. I would go over to his house every now and then, but it wasn't really for him. It was for my grandma, who lived next door to him and my two younger siblings on that side. I never really got to have a relationship with my dad because of his lack of presence in my life.

I will say my siblings on that side have a different outlook on my father, because up until they were removed from his home, he did attempt to do the 'single dad' life, with assistance from their grandparents, of course. I respect him for that. Their mother was in prison, and it was that or his kids would be taken away. Even though they were eventually taken from him, he at least tried. That says a lot about him. I feel that if my mother hadn't been able to be raise me, he would probably have done the same for me.

I genuinely believe my dad cares about me, and over the years, we've been able to communicate through letters about how his lack of presence affected my life. Even though he lived in the same town, when I was of age where I felt I was carrying bitterness about feeling like I didn't have a father, I just couldn't say that to him face-to-face. ,. Writing has always been a way for me to express myself more truthfully, so I wrote him a letter, and wouldn't ya know, I got one back! It was nice to hear his side of things and hear him express how excited he was when he first heard he was going to be a father. The falling out between him and my mother was hard for him. In his letter, he said he did the best he knew how, and isn't that all we can ask of people?

We all stumble through our lives with our own perspective on everything we do and all that happens to us. I think most of us never expect, or even realize how much we hurt the people we care about. Regardless of how I believe my dad should have handled it, he simply didn't see the damage his lack of presence would cause. I accepted his apology, and we were able to hear each other out, agree to disagree, and put it all behind us. I wouldn't say it changed our relationship; more how we viewed it. Now, we talk on birthdays and holidays typically and I'm at a place where that's okay.

On my mother's side, drugs were always around as well. It was normal to just see them around the house. She was the cool mom, the life of the party, the one that let us get away with things. As I got older, she was more like a friend than a mother. We even started smoking pot together at times. Again, that probably went back to what she dealt with as a child. The army-style, boot camp restrictions in her home made her look at discipline in a negative way because of what it did to her. I believe she did what was right in her mind. Maybe she loosened the reins too much, but again she didn't know any better.

Whether we recognize it or not, those early lessons stay with us all our lives. I guess the lack of male attention when I was growing up created this void that I needed to have filled. Different father figures coming and going, getting attached to them for just one day, then leaving made me desperate for someone who represented stability. And my future husband seemed to offer everything I had been missing. The attention from him, along with the love and acceptance from his family were both attractive and captivating. I guess you could say I became obsessed with him.

Those who knew me during that awful time can attest to what I am talking about. I needed to constantly have him around. I would grow anxious if I could not get a hold of him immediately. I would be emotionally devastated if I felt like he didn't want to be with me, even for a little while. I was clingy and desperate, because I was so afraid that he would wake up one day and realize that I was not worthy of his love. It's embarrassing now, but how many people feel like that to some degree?

Being alone with my thoughts only made it worse. I would beg him not to leave me, even when I did nothing wrong. I would avoid speaking my mind or expressing how I really felt out of fear it would cause an argument or convince him to leave. I would rather not have a voice at all than to speak and get it wrong. So, I chose to be silent, rather than risk the possibility of losing him. Talk about toxic! For example, there was a time while we were dating that he did break up with me, but I refused to accept it. I continued to pursue him even while he went on dates and openly flirted with other girls. I made it clear to him that I knew he was supposed to be my husband, and I would wait for him until he knew it too, no matter what.

Daddy issues, to say the least!

I felt like I had to earn his love or prove to him I was worth it. It was a more subtle type of addiction than substance abuse, but every bit as powerful. I ended up tolerating things I shouldn't have. What I had with him felt better than the loneliness I felt growing up, so I ignored all the red flags that started to show up as time passed. Maybe I was stupid, but I was at such an impressionable age, I guess I didn't know any better.

Or maybe I did.

Maybe I just didn't want to risk losing this newer, more expressive version of family than I had been used to. In my mind, a desperate, self-smothering love was better than no love at all. I was still attending the alternative school while we were dating and even though I knew what I had done to get there, I felt I didn't belong in that place, and ended up dropping out of school in the eighth grade. Being with him was all that I wanted. I didn't care about anything else. I remember avoiding any situation that would cause him to question our relationship; to the ridiculous degree that when asked who my celebrity crush was, I wouldn't answer, afraid I might be disrespecting him or going to get him upset. Even the times when other men would hit on me, I blamed myself. I felt it was my fault and that I was probably staring at them first, or somehow gave off the wrong signals. I would try to avoid any even slightly uncomfortable situation, just to keep us together, whatever cost!

Our relationship moved very fast. One reason was that the church had a way of pushing hard on the idea of marriage, especially if they know you were struggling with sex. Sure, we all struggle with sin everyday…lying, gossiping and even worse things now and then, but that's a whole different conversation. The church saw marriage as a way to keep young people from getting into trouble or ending up in a situation they couldn't handle.

Even though I was young, I was also already considering marriage, because I was having a hard time changing a lifestyle in an environment that was conducive to the changes I was hoping to make. I mean I was fifteen and he was nineteen. I couldn't just move in with him. I mean, I guess I could have, but the way it would have looked to the church and to his family would be that we were not doing anything but "shacking up."

To win him over to the idea, I grew more focused on becoming everything he wanted me to be, while slowly losing what little bit of myself I had at that age, in hope that I might be able to change his mind. I put him on a pedestal, tried everything I could to have him see me as the perfect future wife for him. With being introduced to God and him at the same time, a loving, all-powerful father figure that could change my life for the better, I felt that I let him take some of God's place in my life.

I'm sure was as toxic for him as it was for me to view him so highly. After all, he's human and it was inevitable that he was going to let me down at some point. It might be a small disappoint or a soul-crushing collapse of everything I was coming to believe in.

But I'm getting ahead of myself....

This whole Christian lifestyle was so new and foreign to me. The idea of two loving and involved parents seemed like heaven to me. As I said before, I was raised by a single mother struggling to bring up five kids on her own. She did the best she could with what she knew, and I'll always be thankful for her. She kept us clothed and fed, and we always had a roof over our heads. I can say my siblings and I never went without anything we needed. She is by far one of the strongest women I know! Yes, she may have made some bad choices, but don't we all? And yea, if you are wondering she did have to sign for me to get married at fifteen, but I really didn't give her much choice. Remember the obsession and unhealthy attachment I mentioned? I stayed after her about it and wouldn't let up. And she obviously saw the positive changes I was making since being with this new man in my life. I mean, I was going to church, I quit smoking, quit drinking and doing drugs. I even took out some of my piercings.

As a mother, I probably would have thought it was for the best for a daughter as wild and uncontrollable, as I had been when I was younger. I do feel it was for the best, considering what would have been if I had continued to live my life running the streets.

But I do feel my mom loved me the only way she knew how, and I can't fault her for something she didn't know how to do properly. Nobody has all the answers when they become a parent, especially if you have a difficult childhood yourself. It hurt me to hear stories of how my mom was raised, because she went through even more than I did. Nobody taught her the best way to deal with kids, so she did the best she could with the situation and the tools she was given. And remember that I wasn't the easiest child to deal with. Still, I appreciate her effort and will always be thankful for her regardless.

And for the record I don't regret getting married. I regret some of the customs that we adapted to during marriage. I regret not giving myself time to grow and develop as a child and to figure out who I was before changing myself into what everyone else wanted and expected me to be. I regret idolizing the image of my husband over the reality. I regret not loving myself enough, but we will get to that as well.

As my wedding day approached, I was beyond excited. Everything had happened so perfectly. From finding a wedding dress just my size at the Goodwill for $50.00 to his dad knowing a lawyer who signed our marriage license on the hood of his car on his off day at a gas station. It was just all falling into place so effortlessly. I felt so sure of my decision. This was exactly how I thought this moment was supposed to be. Keep in mind that I was still a child, not really knowing what I was doing. In my head, I would get to live with this perfect guy that I am in love with, and then have sex guilt-free. A real win-win, right? I remember getting ready and having all my siblings there, even the ones from my dad's side. And I was surprised when he showed up too. Last minute, but he was there. My wedding day is the one and only important event in my life that my dad has ever come to. No birthdays, no graduations, but at least he was there on my wedding day.

It was a beautiful August day. The sun was shining in that perfect blue sky with puffy white clouds. My new husband's father was a preacher, and we were married by his dad under the pavilion of the church we were attending. I remember standing there, feeling like the luckiest woman in the world. I didn't care what anyone thought about what I was doing or how fast it all happened. I had never felt so sure about anything up to that point.

The ceremony was beautiful. We said our vows, and I meant every word. We exchanged a kiss and then turned to the crowd for the first time as a Mr. and Mrs. My heart was so full. I felt I had everything I would ever need in life, because I had him.

Our wedding reception was full of family, laughter and fun. After it was over, we headed to our honeymoon in Gatlinburg, Tennessee to celebrate being husband and wife.

After such a hard childhood, my life was turning into a perfect little fairy tale. But I had no idea what was to follow.

Five
Motherhood

And so, at fifteen years old, I had a husband, a growing faith and hope for a better life.

My new husband and I had decided very early on to start a family. That's what was expected of us, and what we expected of each other. We really didn't even understand the weight that it carried, more like we went off with the fantasy of it all. When I say early on, I mean our honeymoon was exactly a year from our first date. You know, the first comes love then comes marriage, then comes a baby in a baby carriage. That was what we were supposed to do, just the next step after the wedding.

I was pregnant and had our first child at sixteen.

There I was, a child raising a child, trying to figure out who I was, struggling to adjust to adulthood and responsibility, trying to understand my role as a wife, and a godly one at that. At the same time, I still wanted to be a kid and stay out at game nights, do prank call, and all the things that a kid would be doing as a young teen. Instead, I was at home, rocking a colic baby, and doing my best to fit into this new life that I had never really seen modeled out for me the correct way.

Your girl was winging it big time!

We named our daughter Krislyn, a name given to me from a dream I had while pregnant. From the moment she was born and placed in my arms, I felt my life finally had meaning. Krislyn looked up at me and I knew I was supposed to be her mom. To go from existing solely for my husband to seeing my reflection in the soft, gentle eyes of a little someone that was now fully my responsibility was both frightening and completely liberating. This tiny infant filled my life with so much purpose and honestly gave me a reason to fight as hard as I do, even to this day.

I didn't have many friends at this point because I was told the friends I had before weren't “good” for me, and I didn’t know how to stay friends with people who weren't trying to live the same drug-free, spiritually life I had now. This was especially true for my guy friends, so I had cut a lot of people out of my life.

But I had my husband, and now I had this precious child. What Krislyn will probably never know is that she was my strength on my loneliest days. We did everything together. She was my mini-me. All I wanted was to make sure she was safe and happy and would have a better childhood than I had. We put her in everything. From T-ball to gymnastics; basketball, cheerleading and dance; she did it all. She was good at everything she tried. She was my life, along with her father. Making them happy and seeing them smile was everything to me.

I was trying to be so many different things so fast, I never really had the opportunity to just become me as an adult. To become who B is, outside of a role or position in life that was pushed on me. When you are a kid and have things modeled at home, you adapt. If you see a lifestyle dominated by drugs and drinking, you copy it, or take it to even further extremes. If you are never given any space or responsibility, or are always being told what to do, you lose the ability to make decisions for yourself. Years go by, but you stay a kid emotionally, and when the time comes to make some important choices or hard decisions, you question everything about yourself. It becomes easier to sit back and let everyone else make the decisions for you. Even worse, you begin to choose people and situations that shut you down, boss you around and control every detail of your life. It's way too smothering to feel comfortable, but you don't have the courage or the will to live any other way.

There's little difference between everyone telling you what to do as a child and finding yourself in a marriage where you let your husband's voice shape a lot of who you are, or who you imagine you should be. It's just a different voice, leaving you no space to figure out who you really are. You assume all these roles to define yourself and give you a way to deal with others, but soon learn you have left yourself no way to understand who you are inside.

I was a daughter, a mother, a wife and a sister, and each of those roles are important to me. Each of those define a part of me. Each of those help me relate to a small piece of the world…but only in this past year have I come to realize that I have an identity outside of these roles. I have come to understand there is a fully formed person that God created hidden in each of those things, but I am even more than all of them combined.

I haven't fully figured it out yet, but I can see a glimpse of her, eager, searching and scared. Trying to break free of her fears and doubts, in order to be the woman God has in mind for me. And I'm searching and willing to go through the long process to find her!

If your sole identity is found in roles and positions, or even in other people, then what happens when all of those things disappear or fade away?

What are you left with? And an even more important question is… *Who* are you left with?

The answer is YOU!

At the end of the day, you are the only guaranteed person you will have for the rest of your life.

Outside of God, of course.

Unfortunately, people in your life will come and go. Loved ones will pass away. Situations and circumstances we were so sure would last forever, never do. Everything around you changes, but you will always have YOU.

But who are you? Do you even know?

Maybe it's time to take a long, hard look at yourself to see beyond what others have told you to be. Maybe it's time to find the REAL YOU, the TOTAL YOU that's hiding deep inside, aching to be seen…

And dying to get out.

Six

Realizations

As I write this, I am thirty-one-years-old and only now realizing I have to figure out who I am, outside of what everyone else needs me to be.

Part of figuring that out means asking yourself a lot of questions:

What do I want for myself?

What do I enjoy?

What are things I don't like?

What are my passions?

What are my values?

What are boundaries that I need to set, and for what reason?

What are my goals? Are they the same as when I was younger?

And what do I need from me to make me feel whole?

That's another list that could literally go on and on. As you ask yourself each of these questions, try to see whether they are really your thoughts and answers, or simply things that other people told you to say. Your parents, your friends, your community, your teachers, and even people who hurt you, all have had a role in making you believe certain things and molding you into who you are today.

And that's not always bad.

We learn from others. We adopt what we hope are good habits and ideas worth following, then we use them to build our personalities from the inside out.

But too often, we give someone else too much power over our lives, and the person they shape us into is nothing more than a shadowy reflection of that other person. We are taught to be blurry copies of our parents. To be accepted, we mimic our friends in the way they talk and the things they like. When we are scared, we try to act tougher or less concerned than we really are. If we are afraid someone will hurt or leave us, we act like someone who doesn't care at all (even when we really do.)

We create dozens of mirror images to please other people; subconscious reflections that may have little connection to who we really want to be in our hearts.

That's why it's so important to take some time for yourself every so often. To really look at whether the face you put on for others is your true face…or just a mask you were told to wear, or a lie we internalize to make them feel more comfortable

Something else I realized is that you can't love someone you don't know. I mean you could, but you wouldn't do it right or get very far. So until you get to the bottom of you, until you take the time to really get to know you, you will never be able to love yourself in an effective way.

The way you deserve. The way you need to be loved.

**If you don't love yourself properly,
you set the bar even lower for
how you expect others to treat you.**

If you take a minute and evaluate some of the ways you've been treated, you can usually see how they were just reflecting the way you felt about yourself! This also can be applied to how we give love to others.

God says to love our neighbors as ourselves, but if you don't love yourself, does that mean you can't love others properly either?

This takes time and a lot of trial and error to figure out. It takes some hard digging and reflecting, but I encourage you to stretch yourself and give grace to the person you are becoming! The person you have repressed for so long.

Remember that *you are worth it,* and the person you will find on the other side of all this work will be priceless.

I wanna throw religion in at this point, because I feel it shaped some of the most toxic ways of living and mindsets for me. I know, the idea of church being toxic doesn't seem right, but at times, it can be absolutely true!

Many religions have a tendency to make you feel ashamed for struggling. They make you feel like you have to live up to this rule book full of man-made agendas that push shame and condemnation, instead of the love and forgiveness that God offers. Shame and condemnation lead to living a masked, inauthentic life.

But covering up what you are really going through is a form of lying. Lying to yourself and those around you. Because how can you be serving this God and still struggling with sins of the flesh, especially if you are in any type of leadership?

Have you ever met someone who tells you that when you give your heart to God, all your fleshly desires are supposed to just go away? Or that one spark of spiritual grace means you are suddenly supposed to be strong enough to never fall again?

These judgmental religious types make you feel that every time you sin, you're going to hell, unless you immediately repent and get reborn again (and again and again.)

There are some principles like repentance that are correct, but people can bend it with their own self-righteous views, so that the system itself becomes a burden, instead of a blessing. That's such crap, and honestly, why so many people probably turn from God after messing up. It's not God that is condemning them. It's their fellow church members that are making them feel defeated for having moments of weakness, or for being human! Like why would they want to live for someone that has unrealistic expectations? We are all sinners, after all, and not even God expects us to act like saints from day one. That mindset allows no space for transparency and starts the process of covering up who you really are and the areas that need God the most.

I've finally come to realize that it's about a relationship with a God. Period. A God that sees you for exactly for who you are and still chooses you regardless! All the imperfections, all the mess ups, ALL OF IT. He sees them and still loves you!

For so long, I was more focused on following the rules that everyone around me told me I needed to follow. The rules that were shaping my convictions and lifestyle. Rules that if I felt I messed up on, I'd go straight to hell and God would no longer bless me or extend favor on my life. It was a lot of pressure to say the least!

Something I've recently adapted as a mantra from Michael Todd, one of the GOATS (Greatest Of All Times) is *Progression Over Perfection.*

Say it with me...
Progression Over Perfection.

Perfection doesn't exist. If it did, why would God need to send his Son to us, knowing that perfection was obtainable? Jesus came because he knew that we, as humans, fall short every now and then. That's why he felt as comfortable with sinners as with the saints. Trying to do the right thing is as important as always doing it. Is someone who has never known temptation a better person than someone who is severely tempted, but struggles to fight it every day? If we were all destined to be perfect, there would be no need for Jesus to come down. What God expects, what God wants, is that we strive to die daily to our flesh and surrender to Him! That's it. Period!

I'm still shaking off some of that religious crap because of how long I was in it. I am so thankful my heart and mind has been set free, because God is so much more than a rule book to follow.

The church we were involved in early on in our marriage shaped some of the ways I viewed others and their situations. I feel it led me to pick up some religious characteristics. I became a lot more judgmental of people who were struggling. Here's another part I feel ashamed to share, but again, this is part of the growth process. After all, how can I be free from something if I refuse to address and accept it?

I'd say I feel I started to realize it in myself when we started attending a new church about seven years ago. This new church brought to light so many areas that I had wrong. It was full of people that were transparent about where they were, without being shamed. Seeing their acceptance, I started to realize I had picked up some ugly parts to religion. I had been taught to be more concerned about what people showed on the outside than trying to understand the issues they were facing. It was all about what I "thought" their lives as religious people were supposed to look like, instead of trying to understand all the pressures and problems they were going through.

I struggled with getting to know their insides, who they really were, instead of that same mask we were all supposed to wear. I wrestled with loving people correctly. If I knew they were "sinning," I would look down on them, even though I was struggling myself. Which brings me back to my point… that we all sin. Everyday! But I feel religion puts an emphasis on certain sins. Like one is greater than another.

Unfortunately, I had the wrong focus and I've had to humble myself and apologize to a lot of loved ones. People I treated like plagues, because I knew something they were struggling with. I am so thankful God opened my eyes and let me see how He values love and relationships more than rules!

I carried some guilt for a while over how I handled certain situations. Sadly, there are some loved ones that are not here anymore for me to apologize to, and I have no chance to ever make it right. I wish I knew then what I know now. I would never want them to feel any less, because of something I didn't know they were going through, or just because I chose not to see past the surface and into their hearts.

I pray they can forgive me for my judgmental attitude.

The love was always there, it just wasn't always shown the right way. In that moment, I thought I was doing right, but I now see I wasn't. I wish I could have the opportunity to do it all again. To not be 'that person' who condemns others for what she herself is going through. I wish I could make it right, but I can't. Some moments are set in the past and the damage we do can't be undone. I just have to trust that God will use those situations for His purpose.

It definitely taught me some hard, but valuable lessons.

For a very long time I operated out of that judgmental lens. If someone cussed, smoked, drank, had sex outside of marriage, listened to secular music, or even had tattoos, they couldn't possibly have a good relationship with God. As if I forgot where I came from. I would immediately judge and assume things when that wasn't my role to play. It created a bitterness in me. I had a hard time in forgiving others, which made it even harder to forgive the weaknesses I saw in myself. I was heaping on pressure to live up to unrealistic expectations, because I felt God's love and favor had to be earned.

And my bitterness increased, because I was trying so hard, when I felt like others weren't. And so, I became even more harsh and condemning.

Now don't get me twisted. I do feel we should all work out our own convictions, and what may not be okay for some may be okay for another in certain situations. That's not always our place to judge. But at that particular time in my walk with God, I felt there was no way I could ever do any of those things without feeling I was going to hell. Not from a conviction standpoint, but from this rule book that I felt like I had to follow. And that rule book said I couldn't be around anyone that didn't follow it as well.

I was at such an impressionable age, and being taught so many things, that I just assumed this was the way life was supposed to be. You were perfect or God didn't love you. You did everything you were told to do, or no one else would either. You didn't even get close to sin, or you weren't worthy of being loved.

Those first ten years of my marriage were spent juggling life, work, family and ministry. You could only imagine how much masking we started doing; covering up things in fear of judgements, hiding struggles to uphold an image, hearing how things should be modeled at home, but not really seeing it work out. We were both struggling with things in different ways, really just kids trying to figure it all out. When we went through troubles in our marriage, I was taught to hide them, to keep them locked away inside, so tightly, it hurt. The only ones who really knew what was going on were a select few of his family members that tried their best to help. But even though they meant well, and acted out of love, the outcome always came back to us adapting to that same fake persona of what our marriage and our life was supposed to look like, and the cycle would repeat itself too many times to count.

There were "little" things early on that I would notice, but again, I wouldn't say anything just to keep peace. If I did say something, I was made to feel it was either my fault or I was "crazy" and making something up.

The first time I felt the rug completely pulled out from under me was about six years into our marriage. At that point, I honestly believed my husband could no wrong. To me, he was everything a Christian was supposed to be. We were in church every Sunday and very involved in some capacity. From the beginning, he had let me know what was okay and what wasn't. He made the rules, instilled in me the standards, and I followed. The music, the clothes, the piercings, they were all according to his rules, so when he started to veer away from the standards that HE had set, it became confusing to both of us.

We were living in government housing when I found out my husband had been getting high and drinking with some of the younger crowd in the apartments. I was completely blindsided. I had no idea and didn't even think he was capable of such a thing, or why he would even want to live that lifestyle. He had been so critical about things my family were doing and didn't even really like me or our daughter Krislyn around them because of it. To hear about this kind of behavior from my minister, the head of my household, the one who set the bar so high for our family really crushed me. It was hard to know or accept what was true at that point. I had taken his word over other allegations, but they just kept on piling up. There were other allegations that came from that incident that I had to take his word over others. To have to defend someone that had just lied to your face was very hard, but I always tried to give him the benefit of the doubt. I felt in his heart that he was sorry, and I was sure he felt bad for his actions. We kept that secret within our tight niche circle, which only contained his father his stepmom and his sister. I refer to them as our "secret keepers."

No one else knew, especially not my family. My younger siblings all looked up to him, as we were really the only stable thing in their lives at this point, and they were too young to even fully understand. My younger sister had come to me about some things she heard or that she experienced for herself, and I would still try hard to defend him. I would come up with something to let her know it wasn't true and remind her of how great he was, in order to shift the focus off the bad and onto the good. My older siblings did not care for him much, so they were just waiting for him to mess up. My older brother felt he was keeping me from my family. Prior to my marriage, my older brother and I were really close. We pulled up everywhere together. But when

I started changing, even though it was for the better, he didn't like that. I believe he saw my husband as a threat.

I definitely couldn't tell my mom either because she was one of the ones my husband tried to distance me from because of her behavior.

Questions flooded my mind, like: "What would everyone think if they really knew?" "Would this change how everyone saw him?" "Would it change how everyone saw us?" He had been this preacher boy and set such high expectations for everyone else, so to see him fall in those grips wasn't easy. It was too uncomfortable to figure out how to deal with everyone if it came out, so we decided to just lock it all away and move past it. I chose to forgive him for lying and doing all those things behind my back. I pushed all those feelings of anger and betrayal down deep inside. Pretended I didn't feel them. Pretended they weren't there. But you can only pretend for so long.

We were always affectionate in our marriage, and it did not affect our sex life, because it was instilled in me that if you didn't take care of your man, someone else will. A cold marriage bed would open the door to pornography, which was something else we wrestled with in our marriage. The pressure always seemed to be tied to what I did or didn't do. I felt if he chose to look at porn, it was because I was somehow lacking in the bedroom. It was a lot of pressure and just affirmed in me that love and loyalty must be earned and was tied to what you can do for someone. Crazy, I know, but I was desperate to be there for my husband, and not be the cause for his failings.

But no matter what I did, the pattern continued. A few months would pass and there we would be, sitting in front of his father again, reliving the same problems over and over again. His dad played so many roles in our life. Our pastor, our source of income, since he was his boss, our counselor, and a primary "secret keeper."

My husband was struggling with smoking pot or taking pills and had been hiding it again. We talked about it, and once more decided again to just move past it and go forward. Keep in mind that all this is going on behind the scenes of a very active ministry, Whether it was a youth leadership position, worship leader, or him just preaching every now and then, these sins could not come out. We did church very well. A few years of dealing with the continuous lies regarding smoking, dipping, pills, drinking, and even a few "flirting" instances where I found text messages that were inappropriate with the opposite sex, kept us in a spiral of alternating good and bad, closeness and distance, forgiveness and resentment. Only our "circle" knew what was really going on, in order to safeguard the ministry and protect the image we had created. Maybe protecting him also protected me. Protected me from a harsh reality I refused to accept. But I didn't realize how protecting him was killing me, little by little. With every lie and every secret, I was losing faith in the one that had brought me to it. Slowly losing security and trust in the man and the belief structure that had rescued me from my previous wild lifestyle.

I started to grow bitter and less empathetic. When you deal with the same instances of shame, guilt and betrayal over and over again, it's easy to lose a sense of your compassion. You begin to recognize that repeated failings are no longer an accident, but a choice. Going to church and putting on a show is what we were good at, but at some point, the show becomes more important than the church. I'm not saying our love for God was fake for either of us. We both loved God with all our hearts, but our lives were not surrendered or submitted to Him. We still clung to things that made us comfortable. My husband's ways to cope with whatever internal wars he was facing, along with my lying and hiding it, were feeble attempts to try and control the narrative of what I wanted and desired, even when it was clear I wasn't in control at all. It's sad that we viewed the church as somewhere that we could be used, but not somewhere we could come and be real and honest about what's really going on and get the help that we so desperately needed. As if God didn't know what was going on in our marriage. As if we could hide it from Him. But we tried for a very long time. Every lie, every secret chipped away my sense of trust. Growing numb became part of my normal. I was no longer as shocked when I found out something new. I started to question his character. At the end of each day, I began to wonder if I even really knew the man I married. And did he even know the amount of pain, resentment and disillusionment his wife held in her heart?

Maybe he had picked up some of these characteristics of what they said he was "supposed" to be from his own childhood. When he was younger, his dad was a preacher and there were allegations that his dad had cheated on his mom. He had a front row seat to watch his family fall apart, to see people he looked up to the most change everything about what was normal to him. One day his parents were leading a church, and a short time later, he saw his mother start drinking and hanging out at bars and then witnessed his dad struggle with some pretty heavy drugs. Maybe it's understandable he might have his own struggles with right and wrong.

Or maybe it was that I was looking past who my husband really was, and trying to make him into someone I imagined he should be and hold him to a standard I thought he wanted? But every situation became just another mountain to get over. Something else to force another counseling session with his dad before sweeping it under the rug with everything else, trying really hard not to bring it up again, so that I wouldn't be seen as the condemning or judgmental wife.

But there was one situation that became too much to ignore. I had sensed something being off for some time now, but when I would question it, I was told I was 'trippin' and letting the past get to me. You can only have your gut instinct undermined for so long, until you know you're not crazy. We had gotten to a place where I kept drug tests and a breathalyzer on hand because I couldn't take his lies anymore. I was sick of having to take his word for it when I didn't believe him. It was tormenting. Even on those rare occasions when he was telling the truth, I couldn't believe him because I had no trust left in me at all. That was my life. My secret life. To everyone else, I would praise him and talk up our marriage as if we were the 'goal' for others to strive for. And yes, I think there were parts of our marriage that were worth it. The fact that we were so young when we got married and still fighting for our marriage, rather than giving up is huge. Nowadays people seem to throw commitment away after a year or two. But we fought for ours. Fought hard. We had gone a little bit where things seemed okay, but I started to feel something was "off." He had been leaving for work really early each day, which was unusual. So, to ease my mind I told him I wanted to go to work with him. I knew that would be fine because he worked with his dad, who would understand my reason behind it. I wanted to assure myself that everything was okay.

But it wasn't.

I guess he knew he was about to get exposed, so he finally admitted that he had been going to a methadone clinic before work behind my back for the last year. A WHOLE YEAR. Spending our money and lying to me every day for A YEAR. I was devastated and didn't know how we were going to get past this one. I knew it was going to take more than just another sit down with his dad. I couldn't keep doing this. It wasn't fair. I loved him so much and just wanted to hold our family together, to get through all this and be what everyone thought we were. To be this image I had created of what I believed we were.

From there, we both agreed my husband needed professional help.

I do want to add that every time something did get exposed, he did show remorse. I knew his apology was sincere. What softened my heart was that he did feel genuinely sorry and that he never meant to hurt me. He didn't mean for his struggle to be tied to my pain. But in a real relationship, we never suffer alone.

His sister was now married, and her husband had joined our "secret keeper" group. He was familiar with a program that could help my husband with his addiction, a place he would have to stay while going through recovery.

This was going to be hard for everyone involved because, regardless of all the struggles my husband dealt with, he was home every night. I never had to worry about that, thankfully. He was a great father and very involved in his kids' lives, and like I said earlier, helped raise his nephew and cousin as well. He was a man with a big heart, which helped offset his big problems. Keep in mind our daughter was getting older and still knew nothing of what we were going through. Imagine realizing your knight in shining armor wasn't as strong as he portrayed. We did a good job at hiding because we thought we were protecting everyone, but maybe, we were only protecting ourselves. Once the curtain was finally pulled down, I don't know if hiding was the best decision.

But we were at a point where we were desperate for change. I know I was. I didn't want to keep living this way. It was too much and causing too much damage. So, he went away for an extended rehab, but only lasted one day. He said it was too hard to be away from his family. I have to admit, part of me was relieved because I missed him so much, yet another part was discouraged, because I knew without his going into recovery, nothing would change.

Here's my journal entry from when I first heard he was leaving the program:

Well…what a day. My husband came home from the program, and I feel I'm realizing how big this giant really is, but my God is bigger! I know without a doubt that God can do anything and everything. But I am so hurt! I feel betrayed and lied too again! I need you to heal me Lord so that I can be what my husband needs to get through this and finally have victory! The devil's time is up, I will not give up my marriage without a fight. You've awakened a beast! I pray for his pain and ask that you strengthen my husband and as he gets strength it will strengthen me! I love you, Lord regardless. You are still worthy! I HATE the devil. I rebuke him! Lord, I'm desperate for you, for a word, I need you! I cry out to you mighty God, awaken the sleeping warrior inside my husband! Build his faith in the Lord. I love you and need you so bad. Please show me and help me be what I need to be. Amen.

I feel my religious ways back then put too much emphasis on blaming the enemy and what he was doing, but what I've only recently realized is that most of what was going on was because of decisions we had made. Those consequences were a result of our choices, things we had done and things we chose not to deal with in an honest, productive manner. Sometimes we give the devil too much credit, or maybe even blame God rather than being honest with ourselves and accepting all the turmoil we are creating for ourselves. Time, prayer and therapy have helped me see that it was our choices that got us where we were. Owning up to that is the first big step in setting things right.

After my husband dropped out of rehab, we decided that the next best option was for him to move in with his sister and brother-in-law, who was actually the director of a drug rehabilitation program and had walked through something similar himself. He could relate. At least I could talk to him and see him throughout this process. It was hard to watch my husband go through withdrawals and hear about how much pain he was in. That process lasted for like a week or two, and I hated it almost as much as my husband did! As days passed, and I realized we were getting closer to his freedom from this addiction, I realized I didn't have much room to express myself and how I felt. It felt selfish to consider my feelings in all this, but it was hard to suppress the feeling that he had lied to my face repeatedly for a whole year. For twelve months, he had made me feel crazy for even questioning his behavior. Everyone's focus was him, as it should be, but what about me? What about the hurt I was feeling? How was I going to be able to trust him ever again after so many lies? What about the weight of having to keep yet another secret? As much as I wanted it to be all about his victory, I felt defeated. But again, the only answer was to shove everything deep inside, sweep it all under the rug, keep even more secrets and continue on.

Don't get me wrong. It wasn't all bad. That's not the image I want you to walk away with. I loved my husband and I know he loved me in his own way. We were just two broken kids that had no idea what we were doing and just trying to do our best. We would be okay for a little bit, trying hard to be kind to each other, only to find ourselves slipping back into the same old patterns of yelling and toxic behavior. Situation after situation would have me hiding within this brittle shell I had built for myself, hating the thoughts and the fears I kept pressed so tightly inside.

I always felt I had to suppress my feelings because of the image we were trying to uphold. Every church we went to, we were in some type of leadership position. We preached God's forgiveness, but I wouldn't allow myself to feel it deep inside or truly extend it. I felt I had to keep secrets. I never got to authentically express what I really thought from certain situations because, heaven forbid, we couldn't let anyone know what was really going on.

To be honest, we probably shouldn't have been in any type of leadership until we figured out how to follow first and submit to God's plan for us. How to be transparent and have accountability outside of family members. I became so good at only showing what I wanted people to see, saying all the right things to make our marriage and our ministry look better, while inside I was still so torn and conflicted. It made me feel like a fraud. On the outside, we seemed great, and I feel that had a lot to do with us having similar passions and interests. We were both competitive, athletic and people thought we were fun to be around. We both loved God, had a heart for youth, with a sincere desire to help kids. We supported each other in helping raise kids that were not ours. My siblings were with us a lot when they were young, and so were his nephew and cousin. Fortunately, they never knew what was really going on behind the scenes.

My husband and I really grew up together. We knew everything about each other, the good and the bad, but started getting to a place where we mastered how to portray what we needed, rather than reveal the truth of all the things we lacked.

The saddest part of masking is that there are so many underlying issues you spend all your energy trying to cover up, even to yourself. Little by little, you try to fool yourself into thinking that everything is okay, until one day, it's just not. It's anything but okay, and then you hate yourself even more for lying about it to everyone. You feel trapped by a toxic mindset that makes you feel that you can't ever be real; a way of thinking that forces you to lie and hide things just to keep your 'perfect' image intact. But you are scared to let go of that image because of the judgement and condemnation that comes with it if you refuse. The same kind of judgement and condemnation you start to throw on other people, hoping they won't see the same flaws in you.

That constant deception and role-playing led to the most devastating news of my life.

Seven
The Worst Year of My Life

It was the end of 2016, when my older brother passed from an overdose. Growing up, Timmy and I were inseparable. We played together, ran together, goofed off together. Throughout our childhood we went through a lot of the same things, so we just had this understanding. All the moving around and sharing rooms and making the most of whatever situation we were in made us lean on each other even more.

Sometimes, when I look back, I wonder how I would have made it without his company.

Like I said, my older sister lived with my grandparents, so it was just me and him and me for a while, at least until my younger two siblings came along. I thank God that when Child Protective Services took us away from my mom, they decided not to separate me and my brother. Timmy was the only familiar thing I had during that time. He looked out for me, and I never had to worry about anyone messing with me, that's for sure. He made friends everywhere we went. That boy didn't know a stranger. He embodied popularity and just carried this presence around with him. I can't think of one person that didn't like being around my brother.

He and I would play with GI Joes to pass time, until we grew out of that. We would play outside, wrestle around, play basketball, and just be kids together. Timmy was really good at football. He received so many awards that mom really didn't have to do much because the coaches wanted him so bad that they helped us financially and with transportation. That was until he broke his thumb in a game. Shortly after that, we were introduced to some things that we shouldn't have. We started partying hard, drinking, doing drugs, and all the things that come with that lifestyle. But through it all, Timmy and I stayed best friends.

To be around Timmy was to laugh, not just your basic laugh, but a full-on laugh 'til you cry. The kind of laugh that feels like a workout, because your sides would ache that bad. He was hilarious.

I have some regrets when it comes to how I treated Timmy when I first started dating my husband. Like I said, he didn't really like me having Timmy around because of the difference in our new, more disciplined lifestyle. On top of that, Timmy's wild friends were always around. He was fun and popular, so he always had someone tagging along. Once I got a little older, we were able to repair the disconnect that happened after I got married. When he would get locked up (which was a lot) we would write letters and I would go visit him in jail. We were able to rebuild from there. The dynamic of our relationship had changed, but the love remained the same. He will always hold a special place in my heart and always will.

When he passed away, I thought I would never laugh again. Even today, I still miss him so much.

Timmy was the second sibling I have had to bury. It's hard to describe the level of grief when you lose a brother and sister before their time. I've had to grieve and cling to every ounce of faith in my being, just to understand why. Why does God take some young, and let others live long, healthy lives? And why did it have to be Timmy or Samantha?

That news was crippling, but 2016 wasn't done with me yet. Only one month later, I was hit with the news that my husband had cheated. The news I don't think anyone expects, or is ever prepared for, came crashing down on me. Of course, things had happened in our marriage that hit me pretty hard, but nothing felt like this. Out of everything wrong in our marriage, this was the one thing I thought for sure I could say would never happen. I'd like to think he didn't think it would either, but suddenly, there we were, sitting in a situation neither of us ever expected. What made it worse was that we had just welcomed our second child. EmJay had just turned one, and Krislyn, our eldest daughter was now eleven.

Between the loss of Timmy and the shock of the affair, 2016 was one of my lowest points in my entire life, both mentally and emotionally. I began to question EVERYTHING I had come to believe, and for the first time realized that divorce was now an option according to the Bible.

But knowing that released a flood of questions, the biggest being, 'Now what?'

I sat on my feelings for two months after finding out the news. The holidays were approaching, and I felt lost and confused, as you can see by these entries in my journal at the time:

December 16, 2016

Lord, I come to you broken, more broken than I ever have been in my life. If only I knew how different my life would be since my last journal entry. I'm so hurt, angry and confused. My husband cheated on me, Lord. Just saying that hurts me to the depths of my soul!

My one person, the person I put so much of myself into, has betrayed me, my family and my trust. I don't understand how this happened? Why or how he could do this to me!? I don't understand, Lord. I feel I cannot bear this. I'm not built for this. I've been through a lot but nothing compares to this.

I feel as though my purpose in life is gone! I lost my genuine happiness. I feel like, if he was capable of causing so much pain to me, what else can he do? I sit and wonder how.

God, please fill this void that he lacked to keep us safe! I'm beyond broken, God. I don't know what to do, or where to go. At times I feel my kids are the only thing that keeps me going. My family was everything I feel it won't work without him. He's the father of my kids. We've been through so much. He knows me, inside and out. How could he hurt me so severely?? How did he do this to our kids and our family?

Lord, please give me strength. I don't feel I can do this alone. I don't know if I'm willing to love him like I once did, in fear of what he could do to me again. How does a person destroy someone they are supposed to have loved? I'm filled with uncertainty and confusion, God. I feel alone, like no one understands, no one can relate.

I've always had to be strong and act like a Christian and do the right thing. Be the bigger person! I can't do that anymore, God. I feel weak, I feel abandoned. I feel alone. I feel hurt. I feel betrayed. I feel disrespected and like nothing.

How does a person pick up from here? How does a person ever trust again, or feel happy, Lord?

Please, help me! I don't know what else to do! I'm desperate for you to help me! I need you more than ever. I don't know what to do, God. I struggle with anger and bitterness and wanting revenge and not trusting anything at all. It's horrible to live like this. I don't think I can do it!

Send me comfort, God. PLEASE!

Rereading that journal entry does bring a lot of emotions to the surface. The pain, the confusion, the emotions were overwhelming. All I could do was plead with God to help me, to come and put the pieces from this broken mess back together again. My whole identity was wrapped up in my husband and this image of us as the perfect, faithful couple. Now that was gone. I felt I had nothing else. There was nothing for 'just me,' outside of those roles.

Honestly, I have to be careful and intentional on how I let myself view this process. Re-reading that entry, I could see that I was crying out and pleading with God, all while my actions stayed stagnant. I wanted God to do all the work, to just make everything better for me. While I was already hurting, I would self-sabotage by pulling out photo albums, trying to relive moments when everything seemed to make sense. I would find his shirts of and hold them and smell them… (Please, don't judge, or act like you ain't never done something ridiculous when you were hurting.) I would message the woman he had the affair with to get details, and then re-read them over and over. I would play sad songs that kept my feelings at the forefront, just pressing on that bleeding wound. But never during that entire process did I take any positive action on my own. I begged God to come in and fix this broken life of mine, while I just kept getting in his way.

We put a lot on God at times. We can dump all our expectations and excuses on Him.

There comes a point that we have to participate in the process.

We have to stand up, even if it hurts. No, *especially* when it hurts. Remember, God rolled the stone away, but Jesus had to walk out. He gives us the opportunity to make the decision. He does His part, but He also wants us to do ours. I wish I could say I knew then what I know now, but I didn't.

Now I'm sure you are wondering if that was it, if that's what led to my decision on divorce. Not yet. But hang with me, and it'll all make sense soon.

I did decide to separate from him and from that situation, but I made that decision for the wrong reasons. Not from wanting to heal, but out of anger, bitterness, rejection, abandonment and embarrassment. Deep down, a part of me still wanted to be with him and just prayed that things could go back to the way they were. Back to when they made some kind of sense. Back to before I felt so completely worthless. Back to before I questioned everything I clung to so desperately. Back to before I felt this insecure.

Back to before that terrible, soul-crushing pain!

Even now, I am embarrassed to admit that I still wanted to be with someone who literally broke me and gave half of me away to someone he barely knew! I felt there would be no way I'd ever get over him. No way I could live my life without him.

He was all I had ever known. I had been with him since I was fourteen years old. He saved me and he defined me. I had let him take some of God's role in my life, to the point that he was the source of my happiness, my purpose, and my security. He showed me a world better than the partying and the streets. At that point in my life, I didn't really know anything else. I didn't have much of a family of my own, and his family was mine. The whole situation just seemed too tangled to even think of unraveling.

Even though I felt crushed and helpless, I felt in that moment that I would never be able to move on from this. I would never be able to love again, never be able to be with anyone else. My life was shattered, but I felt backed into a corner! I was so messed up mentally from the sudden shift my life had taken, that I wrestled with that little girl inside, and her unhealthy attachments and abandonment issues. The scared child who still wanted to stay with him, no matter what he did, or continued to do to me. But then there was that other me. The embarrassed, devastated wife and mother, the woman that was angry, hurt and felt that she deserved better. I was constantly shifting between these two sides of myself, and they were slowly tearing me apart.

This was something I couldn't keep secret. My emotions were not strong enough. This one punked me. My daughter and siblings watched me cry and go through hell, mentally and emotionally. They were just as shocked as I was. My kids' two parent household had now become one, and my daughter had to watch her mother cry, day in and day out, doing the bare minimum to survive. I couldn't even imagine what was going on in her mind or how she felt.

We obviously couldn't stay together because it would have been too toxic for us both. At that point, I wasn't even sure of what I even wanted. I mean I knew what I wanted, which was him and my family, but I didn't see how that was possible anymore with everything we had been through. There wasn't even much trust left to begin with and then it went downhill from there. He stayed with his dad for a little bit while we tried to figure out what would come next. Every morning, I would wake up and he wasn't there, that's when reality would hit me all over again. That's when the anxiety was the worst. I would have panic attacks, feeling so alone and helpless. My kids were the only reason I got out of that bed. I went back and forth constantly… a part of me wanted to let go, part wanted to cling desperately to something that was no longer there, no longer real.

And so, my husband left to stay with his dad for a bit, then eventually moved in with his mother.

In the beginning of the separation, I never really expressed my desire to still be with him because of the fear of what that would make me look like, and the fear of knowing it just wouldn't be the same. Once again, I was suppressing how I really felt because of Fear. I had become really good at that.

A part of me wanted him to fight for me, to prove that he made a mistake and was willing to do whatever he could to make it work. And he did that…for a week. But when he wasn't getting the results he wanted, when he wasn't granted immediate forgiveness, I guess he gave up.

I had found out pretty early on that he had already started entertaining other females, even FaceTimed one from another state while staying with his dad. The CSI investigator in me found her Instagram and wrote to her. I was trying to defend my marriage, making sure she knew I was still his wife, and that she was FaceTiming my husband. Twisted!

She told me he had told her we were getting a divorce. Glad to be informed. I was the one that was supposed to make that decision, right!? When I questioned him, he would put it back on me, saying, "I thought that's what you wanted?" He would then go on to tell me that it was not what he wants though. But his actions were not lining up with his words. Even if my words were saying 'I wanted a divorce,' because I was speaking from pain, I desperately wanted him to change my mind. I wanted to feel that I wasn't worth losing, that I was someone worth fighting for at all costs.

Ever since we first got together, his family was like my family, and throughout the separation they were really there for me, for which I was beyond grateful. They listened to me cry, held me, helped financially when I needed, and supported my decision, regardless of what it would be. As much as I wanted them to be mine, they were also his. I really do feel they loved me like their own. Being so connected to something that was still so connected to him left them stuck between the unconditional love they have for him, because he was their blood, and the love they had for me from the years we had all been together. I couldn't imagine how hard that must have been to everyone involved, but they were family to both of us.

I wished it didn't feel like they had to choose me or him. That wasn't fair to anyone involved. But there were nights I wouldn't have made it through, if it hadn't been for their love and support.

While we were separated, I found out his niece, who was young and didn't really understand the weight of what was going on, had put a picture of him on her social media and said something along the lines of "My uncle is single y'all! Hit him up!" When I saw it, even those last unbroken pieces left of my heart fell apart. I felt at that moment if she cared anything at all about me, she couldn't have done that. How were my feelings not regarded when she made that decision? I was so upset that I called her mom, which was his sister who I call mine as well. We had become really close and still are to this day. She was my person, the one I always called, the one that was always there. A secret keeper. She was even in the room while I delivered both my babies and honestly couldn't have done it without her. So, of course I called and told her about it. But this time I felt my feelings were just disregarded as she defended her daughter. That hurt even more.

I was so angry. I couldn't believe this is what my life had come to. I don't know how, but she ended up at my house and, with feelings at the forefront, we got into a "light" physical altercation. It was just a few shoves and a lot of yelling, Unfortunately, the kids were present and scared by all this. Not as bad as what I had seen growing up, but it made me even angrier, because I put myself in a position for that to happen.

More than anything, I wished there was a way to turn off my feelings, to just not care and move on! As she stormed out of the house, I laid on the ground and cried, wondering how my life got so messed up. I stayed there on the floor, feeling like I couldn't move. Everything was too heavy…I was too heavy. My feelings flowed out of me like some thick, smothering puddle that I couldn't help but lay in for what felt like hours. I couldn't move. All I could do was think, "Well, here's another relationship with someone I love that is falling apart." I wondered if there was or would ever be anyone in the world that was just FOR ME! Someone to stand up for me, defend me, have my back with no ties to him!

Through it all, my soon-to-be ex-husband's dad was amazing as well. He is definitely one of the strongest men I know, even though he's been through a lot himself. He would come over and let me cry and vent for hours. He became one of my "secret keepers." I told him everything, and he understood my tears and my pain. Shoot, he would even cry with me. Even when I would see him cry, I could hear it in his voice. He was just as broken for me, as he was for his son. That's why he's an amazing father, treating us all like family, and going above and beyond for his kids. I know his love for me was genuine, but the same heart that loved me loved the one that hurt me just as much, if not a little more. The same heart that wanted what was best for me also wanted what was best for him. That was hard because I guess I just wished I could have had someone that was just for me and not having to see things through the lens of family and loving both of us.

Though my other siblings were young at that time, they also did what they could to help me through this difficult time. They weren't even sure what to do, because there really isn't anything anyone could say or do to make it better, but at least they tried. My younger brother has one of the biggest hearts I've ever known. He was about twenty at that time and saw how low I was and not in a good place at all. He knows how much I love to shop, so one day he told me to get up and get ready because he was taking me to the mall. He said he was gonna let me go on a shopping spree with a $500 limit. I was shocked because growing up the way we did, we didn't have relatives to fall back on, so for him to spend that much on me was beyond words. It made me genuinely smile, something I wasn't even sure I was still capable of at that point. He even moved in with me shortly after the separation. Both of my younger siblings kept me company during that dark time. They were just so young, it made it hard for me to let them in completely because I felt I was more of a mother to them than their sister. Even though I deeply appreciated their love and support, I felt it was best not to bring them into my circle of 'secret keepers,' so they weren't aware of everything else that had been going on.

Soon after that, things continued to go downhill. My husband started living his life in a way that I just couldn't handle, especially with everything I was going through, mentally and emotionally. He eventually left his dad's house and moved in with his mother, because his dads wouldn't let him get away with certain things. Even though I loved his mom, I did not tell her everything. It was her son, after all. When she finally found out some of the things her son had struggled with over the last few years, she was shocked. She had no idea, which implies we did a good job at keeping secrets, right?

He had started drinking heavily almost every day, going out, and I even heard about a strip club and a few random hook-ups. This was a completely different life than what we had tried so hard to portray for years, and it was hard for me to hear about. I had set no boundaries and would keep up with everything he was doing. I would hear from his family that while he was drunk, he would cry and say he wanted his wife back and our family back together. But just as before, words aren't always enough. His action told a different story.

In the end, I felt I had no choice but to proceed with the divorce, even though every part of me wished he would just wake up and realize all that he was losing.

Then again, maybe he never realized what he had in the first place.

Eight
Divorce

This next journal entry is from the day we signed our divorce papers:

May 15, 2017

It is settled.

Wow! To think that, if you read the first page of this journal and then flipped to this page, I would tell you no way. That will never happen. I can't believe where my life is right now!

I'M DIVORCED!

I'M DIVORCED!

I can't even say the words without my gut wanting to come right through my throat. I'm beyond shocked, hurt and betrayed. I don't know how he let this happen. I feel like I gave it my all. I left it on the line. I tried to be strong, but I guess some people just don't have what it takes or have the will to fight.

All I know is God's word and it does not lie!

Despite my pain, my doubts, my confusion, God is still on the throne. He is in control. I will trust Him, even when it hurts like hell. I can't stop crying. My marriage has been brought to death, and now I have to give birth to something new! I will hold tight to the word. I will lean on Him, my father, my good father, the one who never leaves or betrays me or hurts me. He has my best interest in mind. Even if I'm not where I'm supposed to be, I will follow him until I am!

I have 100% confidence in the Lord. I will shed tears, I will feel pain, but I will not quit! I will not throw in the towel. I will see this thing through, no matter the valley that gets me there!

Whenever I re-read that entry, I feel a wave of emotions. I feel the sadness, the fear of the future, but I also feel courage to believe, to put hope in the one thing I did know, even then, was true...and that was God! I remember being so confused, still trying to figure out the answers to all my *Why's*. Praying to get some sort of closure. My heart was in this tug of war between past and present, and if I should move on or not. I was stuck! Even though I did legally move on, I never really did, mentally or emotionally. I didn't feel I could. I still felt married, even though it was clear to everyone (but me) that we were not.

Marriage was all I had known for so long that I didn't know how or where to start over again. That was especially true when I considered dating. I never dated correctly as a child, of course, and had no experience as an adult. I was fourteen, when I met the man who would become my ex-husband, and you know how that is. At that age, a lot is based on looks and feelings, with no real process or intentionality behind it.

Not only did I feel alone, I felt I had slipped back in time to being this little girl, the frightened child who was just trying to figure out how to understand all these new feelings and emotions, only now with so much baggage to carry. It was overwhelming. I never began the process of trying to figure out this healing thing and was more focused on the past and all the trauma. Woe was me. I was the poster child for self-pity. I just couldn't seem to wrap my head around what I had been through and was desperate for answers or any type of closure.

As I read that entry, I hear a woman devastated but confused on how this life of hers was so messed up from what SHE thought it should be. She was trying to grasp any hope she could, knowing the word doesn't lie. Hoping she wouldn't lose herself in all this chaos. What she didn't realize was that she was already lost. She didn't even know who she was as an individual, who she was alone. She was trying to look into the future while still reliving the past.

The word I'd use to describe her back then was desperate. Desperate to be loved in a healthy way, desperate for help, desperate for answers. It was a tough season, to be honest. Here I was, watching this life and image I had fought so hard to protect come crashing down around me. I don't even know how I made it through. I was grieving my brother and my failed marriage, while shaking off so much religious garbage, adjusting to being a single mom, and finding myself alone for the first time in my life.

I never tried to take control of my thoughts and emotions. I let them drive me for what felt like an eternity. I knew some of the most powerful verses; you know the ones we tend to rehearse when we go through something but don't know if we can really believe them.

On top of his cheating, there was so much more that went on. I mean, he had a girlfriend at the time. And we even had a situation where the cops had to be called.

It was my daughter's birthday, and because of the divorce and the lifestyle he had fallen into, he really wasn't seeing his children on a regular basis. The kids and I were on our way home from a cookout with our friends, in which we celebrated Krislyn's birthday. I was upset because he wasn't putting forth the kind of effort I believed he should have for his children. Keep in mind I had so much built-up anger and resentment towards him at this time. I showed up at his mother's house, where they stayed and started running my mouth. I was telling him that he needed to at least come tell his daughter Happy Birthday. That was the least he could do. As he was walking out to the car where both my kids and my niece were, I was still letting him have it, making references to how his new girlfriend was only nineteen. As we approached the car, he grabbed me and shoved me up against it, and began yelling in my face. As he had me pinned against the car, I yelled for my daughter to call the cops, and she did. The cops arrived and they arrested him.

Do I feel now that I should have told her to do that? Maybe not. Do I feel he should have put his hands on me like that? Absolutely not. I shouldn't have even been there. I shouldn't have put my kids in a situation where they had to witness that. I'm sure my daughter was as torn as I was the night Greg got arrested, knowing her father 'didn't mean to' hurt me, but also seeing the pain and fear in her mother's eyes.

I shouldn't have tried to make him do what I felt he should have been doing. I still was trying to make him be something I felt he should be. Remember what I said in the beginning about when we let our emotions take the driver's seat? Yeah, that one definitely crashed and burned me that night.

I should have taken a deep breath and remembered that…

Desperate feelings don't spring from rational thinking, and they almost never have your best interest in heart.

We become so hungry to fill this temporary void anyway we can, no matter how much pain it will bring in the future. Looking back, I feel ashamed of myself. I had no sense of self-worth, and it pushed me to make increasingly destructive choices. I remember picking him up to go to the zoo, even while his girlfriend was still living with him, and while he was still drinking and doing drugs. I knew all that, but I didn't care about myself enough to see past the reality of the situation. I was just hoping I could help get him back to the husband I wanted him to be, the increasingly unreal image I had in my head.

Now here's the plot twist I need you to pay close attention to. Two months from when I signed my divorce papers and five months total being separated, I started "dating" my ex-husband, if that's even what you wanna call it.

I know, crazy! But I did. I chose to go back to what was familiar and what I chose to define as 'comfort.' To be honest, I was falling back into the trap of mastering what we want people to see, instead of admitting and accepting what we really feel about things. All those fears I told you about in the beginning surfaced in my divorce. I put on this tough girl face, along with my old 'no way I deserve better' attitude.

While all those things were true, my internal feelings and emotions were the complete opposite. I was hurting so bad it was almost like death. And a big part of me was dying, while the mask was still being present. That's a pain I wouldn't wish on anyone.

I wanted so bad to be with a man I knew, deep down, that I couldn't trust. There's that unhealthy attachment exposing itself again! Wanting to be with someone, regardless of what their actions were telling you. Putting your own wants and desires aside out of fear of being alone.

There were so many reasons why I knew I couldn't do it again, but I did it anyway. I felt it would make me weak, knowing how bad he hurt me, and was still hurting me with some of his decisions. To take him back felt diminishing. But for whatever reason, I got so low and hopeless that I felt it was my only option.

The thought of even trying to move on from him made me anxious and afraid. I couldn't shake that obsession. It seemed impossible. How could I be me without him? How could I be a whole person by myself? I was terrified that I wasn't strong enough.

I felt stuck and that, if I wanted to be with someone, my only option was him. Regardless of the present and the past. Regardless of how I really felt. Regardless of the reality of the situation. Regardless of everything I knew was wrong for me, I decided to slip back into painful familiarity. Because the pain you know has to be less than the pain you are afraid might come down from out of nowhere and crush you completely.

I knew I could be with him, even when it was hard, because I had done it for so long. I was so unsure of myself, and of anyone and anything else, I felt I had no choice but to choose false comfort over the possibility of growth.

It all came to one weekend, when I found out my kids were going to be introduced to a woman that he was dating. If he was taking that step, then in my mind, I was sure I would lose him forever (as if I even had him at that moment anyway). My overwhelming fear made me lose sight of what was already lost. I knew I was the one wronged, but I was willing to pretend everything was fine, or at least tolerable, just so I could keep up the illusion that I had it together. Now, I'm not saying I was a hundred percent innocent, by any means. I'm just expressing how jacked up my mental state was at the time.

I couldn't fathom the thought of my children meeting this other woman. I was still living in the devastation from where my life was back then to having to accept this new change. When she gets introduced, the whole thing becomes too real, too final.

My ragged emotions were driving me, and I remember shooting him a text a few days before they were planning to introduce her and asking:

"What if we could make it work one more time?"

His response was:

"If you are being serious, absolutely."

Try to imagine how awkward this was for both of us. We had been through so much, with barely any healthy communication up to this point.

But again, we moved very fast. In no time, we were back together, pretending that everything was fine. We were always good at pretending.

I'm sure everyone connected to us was just as confused as we were. I gave no regard to my daughter and how she felt, and how confused she must have been. I'm sure she had a million questions but probably didn't even know how to identify them or process everything that was happening. The man that once hung the stars was now tearing her world apart. Seeing her mother cry for days on end, while hearing about her father's struggles with everything he preached against in his ministry. At first, I tried to shield her from things, but that became impossible. Krislyn was always with me, and my feelings were uncontrollably. Do I regret that? ABSOLUTELY! She was not mentally or emotionally mature enough to handle it. Her "normal" was not so normal anymore. When she would try to express herself or ask questions, I would tell her not to bring up the past because we were moving forward. I guess I was teaching her to suppress her emotions too, even though I knew how painful and destructive that had been for me. I projected onto her what was projected onto me, not giving her the space to express how she really felt. That breaks my heart to recognize it, but again the only way to address something is to accept it. I didn't care about anyone other than myself. I had fooled myself into thinking this was what I wanted. I see now how selfish that was.

As a mother, I guess I thought I was doing the right thing. That is how I can extend grace to my own mom over the many mistakes she made when I was growing up. She probably felt she was doing the right thing too. We try our very best to do what's right by our kids, but sometimes what we have been through and everything we feel blurs those lines. I was fighting for our family to be together but had no idea how to make it work this time. I gave no thought to what that process SHOULD look like, or how it could affect everyone else. So, we did what we were always good at; acting like nothing had happened.

That only lasted for a little bit.

Nine

One More Try

In the beginning, I guess you could say it was like a honeymoon stage all over again. We were happy just to be back in that "new" vein. Thanking God for restoration and putting our family back together. Regardless, if I feel this was God's plan, or ours, you know what He says... He works ALL things for our good.

Here's an entry from two months after my divorce:

July 23, 2017

This prayer journal just keeps amazing me. This journey has been a roller coaster, so I'm divorced, yet dating, or whatever you wanna call it, with my ex-husband. It's so crazy how it all worked out and fell into place. It's all God and I am trusting Him. I can't believe there is even a chance for restoration. I thought I was done, that there was no way! Then God steps in! I'm taking it day by day and trusting Him fully. I love you, Lord and I'm grateful!

One thing that I noticed, compared to most of my journal entries, is that it's very short. I've tried to identify why I think that may be. Have you ever been in a situation and when you don't one hundred percent feel confident in what you were saying…so you keep it short and sweet and to the point? I feel I was hoping, with all that was in me, that this was going to be all that I thought it was. But deep down, I knew. I knew there was so much hidden within, and I knew it would eventually start showing up. I had been through so much emotional trauma that I hadn't dealt with, so much that hadn't been addressed. And even though my prayers were hopeful, I knew I wasn't going to be able to act like everything was okay forever.

As expected, that honeymoon phase eventually faded, just like it always does. Only now, we were navigating this new life with so much emotional baggage we had never unpacked. And that baggage was getting too heavy to carry around.

And so, I suppressed my feelings, once again! I felt I would be taking something away from God if I admitted how I was really feeling at times. I wasn't okay with a lot of things that had happened, and felt really messed up from them, but never felt safe enough to express how I felt to anyone. Not to God. Not to myself. I felt if I talked about my pain and disappointment, I would only be bringing more shame to the person that caused it and reminding them of their offense. That would be disregarding this big miracle God had given with the restoration of our marriage. I didn't know how to voice how I really felt without bringing up the past, as if our memory has a control-alt-delete button and we can just erase what we want to forget.

So once again, I put everyone else's needs above my own. It was a thing I wrestled for a while, and it ended up getting me pinned. Slowly, I started to feel I was suffocating. I would get discouraged and wonder if I would ever know what it was like to be genuinely happy, or even just okay again. I felt so broken. I lost my peace, my joy and my happiness. I was just going through the motions. There were so many old issues left unresolved and layering on the new issues was just too much.

Being back in church and getting these prophecies with the ministry thriving had me questioning everything.

Questioning if I had a right to still feel the way I did. Shouldn't I be healed by now? Wasn't that part of God's gift to us? Isn't there a time frame when I should just be 'over it?'

The questions made me feel wrong for still being triggered and having moments which made me feel lost again. If I couldn't get over it, if I couldn't just put it in the past and move on, then something must be wrong with me! I mean, I did know what I was getting myself into when I went back to him, didn't I? I did know what he did and was still doing when I chose to go back anyway. So why did it still hurt so much? Why was I feeling so empty all the time?

Here's a prophecy from a leadership meeting that I was recording for my ex -now-husband-again, because he had to work and couldn't make it. In the meeting, I ended up being called out by the speaker. It was one that I needed to hear so desperately in that moment, and even now, with where I sit today, it still makes so much sense.

December 2, 2018

Labryant Friend:

You have seen massive restoration and God said I'm still not done. There is still restoration that God is sending to your heart from childhood places, tied to childhood spaces of pain. God says He is the God that restores. Your heart has been through massive renovation, like a house that has been gutted out with nothing but the frames left. God said since you have left your heart open, you have allowed Me to gut everything that didn't belong, and now He can restore.

You are not behind. You're on schedule. Stop comparing your story to others. He took you another way, a different path. God allowed you to endure. There is a story you will speak out of that will heal hearts and redeem.

I was trying to cling to every bit of hope to this restoration story for my marriage and felt I'd be kicking God in the butt if I expressed what I was really going through inside. I felt that would seem like I was questioning God and His miracles. But that wasn't fair to me. God knew where I was and knew the end from the beginning.

He had been preparing me for what I didn't expect the whole time.

God does not act impulsively.
He's strategic and intentional.

The verse in Jeremiah that says I have a plan for you expresses He's a planner. He states He has a plan but doesn't tell us what that plan is, and, yes, that can be frustrating! But we have to trust that He has one! He knew I was scared, that I was going to mess up that plan. Scared I was never going to feel okay. Just be broken forever.

It didn't take long before we became very isolated again with everything we were dealing with. We were back to going through the motions, where ministry was booming and everything looked amazing from the outside, even though internally, we were dying.

Ministry is what I feel made it work for as long as it did, but also was the driving factor as to why we pulled out. I got to a place I didn't want to keep leading while feeling like I was fronting. To display I was okay, when I wasn't. It was nothing but a show, and I was the main character. If I am being honest, my marriage never fully felt the same after the first divorce.

From intimacy to the way I viewed him, our marriage as a whole was not good from any angle. I got to a place where I felt I would never get to feel authentically happy again. Never know what it was like to love or be loved the way I desired because of everything we had been through, and everything we neglected to properly deal with together. I grew angry, bitter and on edge most of the time. I became toxic because of it. I have no problem with owning how messed up I was. I grew mean and not a person anyone would ever want to be around! I over analyzed everything, became over critical, and cringed on the edge of my seat, just waiting for something terrible to happen or convincing myself it already had.

Instead of getting into counseling, setting meaningful boundaries and having accountability, we just got remarried within two months of 're-dating,' mostly because we were having sex, and were still trying to live up to the church rules about that. See the pattern? Rules and images take priority over feelings and truth. And so, out of desperation, we jumped straight back into the thing that strangled us…our Ministry.

Now, I don't want anyone to think I am saying ministry is bad. It was only bad because it was not operated truthfully. That was our fault. It became just more collateral damage because we had not properly managed the problems we still had in our relationship and the destructive tendencies from our own childhood traumas. We were simply cycling, yet again. We slipped everything under the rug, until it ended up getting so big that it tripped us up again. From all the triggers that ended up causing me PTSD to the lack of communication and not having anyone I felt safe to be real with, to each new trauma piled on top of the old ones, we were collapsing in on ourselves. We never established any boundaries or what our expectations were while trying to make this thing work. So, the first "trigger" or red flag from being back together was a business trip he went on because he was being celebrated for being a top seller with the new company he was working for. I was super proud of him. He was really turning himself around. He had quit smoking and drinking, and was really trying to do this right, despite everything that was against him.

With everything we had been through and the very fragile trust we were trying to rebuild, I became extremely nervous about this trip. Yet part of me felt that wasn't fair because he deserved it. So, off he went.

There was a night I couldn't get a hold of him. Like all night. I don't think I actually slept at all that night did. I had to get the kids up and ready the next morning, and drop them off where they needed to go, before I went to work. Life had to go on, even though my mind was not there. I was running through every worst-case scenario, from drugs to drinking to imagining him with another woman. I felt sick, I almost couldn't function, but I didn't have a choice. I finally got a call from him around noon the following day. I calmly expressed how worried I had been and asked for an explanation. He told me he and a few of the guys went swimming and he didn't take his phone with him. By the time he got back to the room, he knew I'd be asleep.

I had no reason not to believe him, so I asked him to please, never do that again. Later that day I was invited by another wife of a guy that was on that same trip to take our kids to get ice cream. We were looking for something to do since our men were gone. As we sat and made small talk, the situation was brought up... only the story she heard was very different than the one I was told. She said they had gone bar-hopping, got drunk and and who knows what else? I sat in disbelief. Why would he lie to me again so easily?

I was beyond pissed and couldn't believe that after everything we had gone through, and all the promises, he would do that and then lie about it. I let him know I had found out the truth and didn't talk to him the rest of his trip.

I was so mad...No, I was so hurt. I felt betrayed again.

Everything seemed to resurface, and I sat there wondering 'What now?'

He came home, and since we were in leadership and one of the guys from our church could expose him to our pastor. So, my husband told on himself first. The pastor talked to him and then to me, and I guess I chose to just move forward once again. I mean at this point, even if I was second guessing everything, I was in far too deep to turn around.

And so, we kept on keeping on. The youth ministry was growing at an accelerated rate. I think that was the only time we felt fulfillment. Outside of that, there was nothing really there, but numbness. We would come home from work, and each go off to do our own thing. There were even periods that we were not intimate for six months at a time. Instead of husband and wife, we turned into polite roommates. We did try to create moments we thought would help, only to realize we couldn't ignore the truth this time.

In an attempt to bridge the walls between us, we started to plan a vacation, like one we had never been on before. A family cruise to the Bahamas. We were going to do it big. We got tickets to Atlantis and were just ready to get away from life and our problems for a little while, and hopefully, discover a little bit of happiness again, even if it was just for a week.

When the time came, we left full of excitement. We stayed in a hotel the night prior to boarding the ship in Florida. We were trying to find a balance when it came to drinking.

My husband was never one that could just have a drink or two; it always led to getting drunk. But despite that, we had agreed to a bit of social drinking, and nothing excessively. We were going to be disciplined. He assured me he could do it.

Of course, that didn't happen. Before even getting on the ship the hotel was serving free drinks for some occasion they were celebrating, and it started off great. We were taking it slow, until we met some friendly people. When it was time to head back to the room, my husband said he'd meet me and the kids up there. Along with our two kids, we let Krislyn bring a friend, who was also a member of our youth group. Even though I wasn't happy with him staying behind, I didn't want to come off crazy or critical in front of people we didn't even know.

I went back to the room and got the kids settled down, before getting myself cleaned up and climbing into bed. An hour passed, and I started going back there mentally. Every worst-case scenario started running through my mind. I'm sure the kids could sense I was getting anxious, but I tried to keep it together. When he finally stumbled back into the room, he was wasted. He apparently drank heavily with one of the guys down by the pool. I was so mad and reminded him of our agreement and our boundaries. But he was so far gone, he could barely even sit up. And there were the kids, hearing everything. I was so upset and hurt and angry, I even questioned getting on the ship the next day. His drinking stripped every bit of excitement from me. Something that a few hours ago I was anticipating now became something I was dreading.

I couldn't help myself and began running my mouth. Of course, arguing with someone who is intoxicated never ends well. He ended up choking me that night…the first time he ever put his hands on me to that level. Then he made a comment I don't think I was ready to handle. He said he wished he would have just stayed with Holly, his girlfriend from when we were divorced. That one cut deep. That one I don't think I ever bounced back from until I got in therapy. And the saddest part of all was that he didn't even remember saying it the next day. But my daughter heard it all and was terrified for me because of his aggression and bitterness. I told her everything was going to be okay even though I wasn't so sure myself. I thought about calling the cops that night, but we were about to board a ship in the morning. How could I take this trip away from my kids? We had never done anything like this. And all that money had already been spent. We wouldn't have gotten a refund with a cancellation the night before. So, I sucked it up and went on the cruise for them. For my kids.

The next day he was so hung over, he was not much help at all. He slept any chance he could get, so I felt I was doing all the parenting by myself. I was so angry at him! We barely talked or touched that entire trip. It was terrible. And, of course, all that did was make him turn even more to alcohol. He was drunk most of the trip, but this time secrets couldn't be kept because my daughter was finally seeing it all play out first-hand. I hated it and was on edge, because I had no idea what to expect from him. He had embarrassed me in front of strangers, could barely walk, would spill drinks, and make inappropriate comments about our marriage.

'What marriage?' is what I was thinking.

But for me, the worst part of it all was when my daughter caught him recording a girl that was walking in front of us in a thong bathing suit. She didn't say anything at the moment but told me the first chance she could get. Sure enough, when I got a chance to sneak his phone, there it was. I was devastated. Hurt and embarrassed. And how, as a mother, do I explain that to my daughter?

Of course, he threw it back on me, saying that maybe if I was having sex with him, he wouldn't have to do that. Sex was the farthest thing from my mind. I didn't even want to look at him, let alone touch him after that. Because the ship didn't have internet, he couldn't search for anything so he had to record that video so he could take care of himself. And that was supposed to be my fault.

That vacation ended up bringing so many new issues to deal with back home. I remember sitting on that beach in the most beautiful place I had ever seen… looking out at this breathtaking view and feeling…absolutely nothing! Completely numb. I didn't even take one picture that vacation (and anyone who knows me knows I take a lot of pictures and my stories be poppin'!) From there I felt myself slipping into a deep depression for the first time in my life.

Despite all the issues I had growing up, I can honestly say I never really struggled with depression. I mean, I've gone through some things and been low and sad at times, but this level of low was entirely new to me. As bad as it was, I couldn't see a way out, and didn't feel I even had the energy or strength to look for one. I felt like I was stuck in quicksand and it was hard to breathe, or even stay alive. At that moment, I lost my fight for the first time. I waved my white flag and tapped out. I just couldn't do it anymore.

It was so bad, I began looking into mental health facilities that I could check myself into, anything to just get away from this life. This life that made no sense at all.

The only thing that stopped me from going through with it was my kids. I couldn't go any length of time without being present in their lives. They were the only things that make sense to me.

During that season, we withdrew from leadership of our church. I remember getting to a place where I finally didn't care what anyone thought. We had just returned from a vacation to the Bahamas that was supposed to be the best one of our lives (Isn't it funny how we think if we plan this extravagant vacation, we can just leave all our problems at home and somehow, everything will be better?) That sure didn't happen!

I couldn't continue to put on this act anymore. I couldn't pretend to be okay when I wasn't. Shortly after leaving the ministry at that church, we continued to try and keep our personal ministry afloat. When we first got back together, my husband started writing music pretty heavily. He would share his testimony through lyrics from what God had just brought him through and the things God saved him from. It was powerful. He had always written music but had never recorded or took it to the next level. But after we got remarried, his sister and brother-in-law invested in his dream by paying for his first recording session. And that's when the music ministry he called *Pawn4God* became official. His music is good, and not just because I am biased. He has a gift and an anointing, along with a way with words that really moves you. He began to perform at churches and social events, and soon his music was released on all platforms. Soon *Pawn4God Ministry* also gave birth to *The Pawn Squad*, a youth development program that helps teens that have a desire to use their gifts for God. It didn't matter what kind of gift they had; singing, rapping, spoken word, or whatever...The Pawn Squad would help them grow their talent, along with a heart for God. We would come alongside as mentors and help equip them with the resources they would need. Our heart was to help kids be able to dream big, with no limitations. One of my husband's regrets was waiting until he was in his thirties to start. We helped kids get studio sessions, merchandising, opportunities to perform or speak. We helped them start their own personal ministries, and I want to shout out to Just Different, an amazing podcast hosted by two of my favorite young men. You should check them out. We even took one young performer to Hollywood to record his first music video. We were passionate about helping kids become everything we knew they were capable of. Maybe the passion stemmed from us being so unsure of who we were supposed to be when we were kids, and we didn't want to let anyone else miss the mark. They became our family. We were invested both financially and emotionally. So, with so many others tied to this decision, people that I loved and wanted the best for, I felt like we had no choice but to move in this new direction.

A few months later, we were connected to an organization from an event that we hosted at one of their venues. It was youth-based and seemed appealing. They offered us full-time paid positions to do something we loved, which was to just love on kids in the neighborhood and run the open gym.

Coming out of the ministry at the church we were involved in, which no longer felt like they right thing to do, mentally or emotionally, to now getting paid to do something we love, and were passionate about, seemed too good to be true. And like I said, we had others connected to us from his personal ministry, and this opportunity would benefit them just as much as us. This was a heavy decision.

I felt a lot of external pressure, while feeling dormant, and even dead inside. Still, I agreed to take the position, hopeful it would be fulfilling, and for a brief season in our lives… it was.

Ten

Clarity, At Last

Throughout this whole journey, it's crazy when I can see God's timestamps throughout it. Because without leaving the church ministry shortly after joining another organization, I can say confidently I would not be where I am right now. I needed those connections to recover my spirit and rediscover who I was, and that to me is mind-blowing.

In the moment, I would have sworn that opportunity was just for my husband and all he was offered. I was typically behind the scenes, helping things in more of a manager role. But in truth, it was God intervening for ME! I met some of the greatest people that I still stay heavily connected to from taking that leap of faith. One of them is my mentor, Coach Bibb. He joined that same organization shortly after we did, and I guess you could say our relationship started as him being our supervisor. He would give us direction, while working with us at that organization. He came alongside us and became a voice we could hear. With his encouragement, I started to get some of my old fight back. Through his words, I found the strength to look for a way out of this mess I had fallen into, time and again.

Coach Bibb connected us to a counselor, and this counselor said she felt led to offer us ten FREE sessions for our marriage.

God is just so on time, let me tell you. Despite everything we throw in His way, He always knows what He's doing.

In April of 2020, we started weekly marriage counseling, and honestly, I felt I slowly started getting a little bit of fresh air for the first time in years. I felt I started to pick myself up off the ground, limb by limb.

This counselor didn't see things from a family standpoint but was able to see our hearts just as we were! For the first time, I felt HEARD! I didn't feel bad for feeling the way I did, I felt understood. A few sessions in, I think we both discovered how bad we wished we would have started this process at the start of our rebuilding. But by that point, our 'house' was barely standing, we had attempted to build on something that was unstable. A damaged foundation. We just continued to stacking things up, until it finally collapsed.

In the weeks following, as hard as it was to come to terms with, I realized our marriage was over. As hard as it was to comprehend, it was just as hard as forcing something to work when we just weren't capable of being happy and healthy by staying together. After all that happened, after everything we had done and said to each other over those past years, we had become too toxic for each other.

I want you to hear me, because this wasn't easy to come to terms with, but there will always be things that we don't want to happen, things we just have to accept.

There will always be things we wish we didn't know but will have to learn. People we think we can't live without but will have to let go.

As much as I wanted my marriage to work, I had to accept for us that wasn't going to be our story. And I had to accept that it would be okay.

Again, it was a tough call, mainly because like I said earlier, I felt I was slapping God in the face. There He was bringing us back together just for me to feel I was tearing it apart again. But I never considered God's advice when I sent that text that day. I never consulted him on that decision. I was riding solo, and made a decision that I felt was best, one that made me feel better at that moment, without considering what our future would look like. But God knew the whole time. He wasn't caught off guard. He used that season to teach me so much, and to bring into my life the people and resources I would need to be able to get through it and grow into the person He always wanted me to be.

That is how I am able to sit here today and tell you my story with transparency, confidence, boldness and strength. I had to make a decision I knew would hurt my heart, so that I could heal my soul.

The weeks following my decision to leave the marriage for good were an emotional roller coaster. One part of the day, feeling strong just to be, thirty minutes later, questioning everything! And I mean EVERYTHING! Up and down, and all over the place. Random outbreaks, uncertainty, pain, all the same feelings that were present the first go-around. Only this time, I refused to stay in that self-destructive space. Here I was, divorcing the same man for the second time. Leaving familiarity to journey into the unknown.

Little by little, I began to figure out ways to move forward, to heal, to accept this outcome that I never expected.

This is where I want to challenge you. Where you are at this moment, what you are going through, what are some ways that you can take steps into the direction you want your life to go? Even if they are baby steps, the important thing is to shake off the fears and expectations of others and start moving forward. Setting boundaries and keeping accountability to those boundaries is usually a good place to start.

For me, I had to make it known there would be no conversations about the past with anyone, not even him. It would serve no purpose. I had been stuck for too many years, and I had no time to or go backwards! In the months following my decision, I soon realized closure was not a real thing. Asking for closure is often just an excuse to keep clinging to the whatever shreds of a relationship you can. There was never one answer to any of my million questions about what happened and how I let things get as bad as they did. There was never one simple reason or excuse that would make me feel better.

Why? Because it wouldn't change the reality. I had to accept that truth and figure out ways to process through it.

Well, if you are anything like me, I didn't yet know what direction I wanted to go. I still didn't even know who I was, outside of my identity of being a wife, mother, or someone involved in ministry. Marrying so young, I never really got the chance to become ME. With how messy life was, it would have been overwhelming to even think of the future, I just wanted to make it to tomorrow without losing my mind. All I knew is that I didn't want to feel unhappy and bitter anymore. I wanted to help myself. I wanted to start figuring out how to heal.

For real this time. No fake stuff. No covering up, but really to dig in and move forward.

I just wanted to be genuinely happy.

The first thing I will say is that for me, that meant therapy. The insights therapy gave me about myself and the healing process I would need to go through were a lifesaver. God is so intentional, and when I look back at how it came into my life, I see God all over it.

It started as couples therapy, but I soon realized how much I discovered and uncovered about myself as an individual.

Here's a journal entry from one of our couple's sessions.

May 16, 2020

Wow! I just left couple's counseling. When I first started this journey, my perception was how this process was going to help my marriage and better us as a couple, but now I'm finding out more about myself than I even knew was there. I'm uncovering spaces that I've had covered for so long. I'm becoming aware of why I am the way I am, what it is that makes me 'me,' and who Brittany really is.

Today was big heavy and dark, while bright at the same time, if that makes any sense. I realized I have stronger walls built up than I thought. Walls that took time to put up. Defenses that I've been building long before I even knew what I was doing. I was a child just playing with blocks, thinking I am going to create something beautiful, but ended up being a prisoner to herself! A prison full of brokenness, pain, rejection, and low self-esteem.

These walls cause me to self-sabotage and question my worth, by keeping people at a distance, because at a distance I am better able to control the situation. I can control when I shut the door by never fully letting anyone in! I live in a place where I don't know how to genuinely and authentically have a relationship, because I am afraid of what they really want or what they are trying to do to me.

So I keep everyone at a distance. Wow, the root goes deeper than I thought, all the way back from childhood rejection and abandonment. Never knowing if my mom and dad were on something has caused me to question people's motives and authenticity. It's a miserable, exhausting place to be. Feeling like no one could really love me, even if they say they love me!

I'm too damaged, broken and mean for genuine authentic love! Well, as today exposed this wall/ root that I've had and wasn't aware of, I surrender it to you, Lord, so I can stop self-sabotaging my happiness and my purpose!

I DO DESERVE to be happy! It is possible! I am loved! People do love me for who I am, not what I have to pretend to be! I no longer have to live in a mindset of 'I gotta look out for me, 'cause no one else will.' I don't have to think like that because God goes before me. He loves me. My family loves me. I now know I can't control anyone else. I can't control every situation and circumstance. I can only *control myself* and *my reactions to things.* So today, I take captive every thought of 'not good enough,' every 'not worthy,' and everyone's expectations and I surrender my heart, the dark places that I wasn't aware even existed. I release the thoughts that hold me captive to the hurt and the regrets of the past.

I give them all to you, God!

Therapy gave me space to go to where I felt heard and understood, with no judgement, but with genuine desire to help. Therapy has revealed so many hidden areas of my life that played roles in why I operate the way I do. It enabled me to find the roots to things that bubble up to the surface and helped me begin to work on pulling them up and changing my negative narrative. Being able to talk to someone about how I really feel is freeing. Figuring out my *Why's* is empowering. It establishes a level of confidence within myself. It's a process to learn to trust yourself, even though you've had your gut instinct undermined and pushed down for so long. That doesn't mean you don't listen to others who genuinely have your best interest at heart. But you also have to take that advice and measure it against what you know is right for you. You have to learn to trust yourself to know the difference. And if you fail, as you will, (we are human after all) you have to learn to forgive yourself and keep pushing forward. You have to stick to your word, show up for yourself, find ways to love yourself, to grow and be better. How you love yourself sets the bar for how others will love you, and for how you will be able to love them in return.

I have learned to trust Brittany. To go to bat for Brittany. Fight for her, love her, protect her, help her discover who she is and help her to be her best self every day! I realized that little broken girl that was laying on the ground begging someone to fight for her needed to find the hero within HERSELF. Once again, it is not easy. It's not a one-shot fix. It takes going back into some tough memories, but with the right person to guide you, it's safe to do. And remember, you are not alone this time!

There was one session I will never forget, when I vividly saw myself, my younger self. She was about fourteen or fifteen years old, and she was crying.

My therapist had me start describing exactly what I saw. I was scared to be honest, but I went with it. I described that she was alone, sitting on a concrete floor. The walls around her were concrete as well. It may have been a prison, but could also have been a basement, I wasn't sure. This young, frightened me had long hair, jeans and a black tee, with her head down in her knees. She couldn't see me. She didn't know I was there, but I saw her.

When I started crying, so did she. That's how I knew we were connected. Then she was gone. It felt so real and made me feel crazier than I already thought I was. But from that moment, I realized there was a child in me, hurting and alone, and I needed to get her attention. I needed to let her know I am here, that I will find her, and that I want to help!

Therapy can definitely be scary, but you only get out of it what you are willing to put in. You have to apply yourself and do the hard work. I scheduled a session with my therapist before I started writing the section about the most difficult things I had been through, because I wanted to make sure I was speaking from a position of healing, not hurting. I wanted to be clear that I forgave my ex-husband, and I pray he forgives me for my part in our marriage dissolving. There was one session when I realized I owed him a phone call with an apology. Therapy not only reveals the strengths and blessings in your life, it can also expose the ugly parts of you as well. Therapy helped me realize the characteristics that I created from not dealing with my suffering over the years gave him no space to be honest in return, no openings to be transparent with me. My judgment and harsh reactions didn't give him the safety to struggle with his own issues. I paid no regard to what he was going through, only focusing on what he was doing to me. I realized I was that toxic church that I talked about in the beginning. I had set unrealistic expectations. I had elevated him to a role that should only be filled by God. In this way, I had set him up for failure and disappointment. That was a heavy realization for me. I know he has a huge heart, and there's a part of me that will always love him because of the impact he had on my life, not just the negative ones. This man saved me. Who knows what my life would have been like if I hadn't met him and his family when I did? Would I have ended up in prison? Would I have died from an overdose? Would I ever have found God, or the strength that has made me the woman I am today?

I'm grateful that this healing I found through therapy, and with the power of God's love, that I am finally able to glimpse the purpose behind it all. To see that, despite it all, God had a plan for me, and everything that happened was another step in that plan. And so I encourage everyone that I meet to find a therapist. I thank God for mine. She is everything I didn't even know I needed. She has a way of seeing you when you feel you are hiding, hearing you when you think you've never been heard or felt understood. She has a way of breaking down everything into clear words and expressing it in a way you haven't been able to articulate before. She has clearly been called to do what she does and I'm so thankful she was obedient to that call!

Never be ashamed or embarrassed to find ways to heal. It takes strength and courage to break generational things off, so that our children and anyone else in our lives do not suffer from something they had no part in.

Side note here; having a therapist is a tangible way to express yourself, but what about those midweek moments when you feel so bottled up and need an outlet? Where you're literally driving yourself crazy? For me, journaling has been a way to get out those thoughts and express myself. As you can see from the moments throughout this book, I've used real 'raw in the moment' truths to bring more of an authentic look to what I was feeling at that very moment.

Sometimes I write for myself, sometimes I write to God, sometimes in the same entry. Sometimes I write as if I'm in front of someone, and then hope and pray no one will ever read it. Either way, I feel writing is a healthy way to release emotions and thoughts, without necessarily needing feedback from anyone, or an answer to my own *Why's*.

The truth is, I'm not big on venting to just anyone and am still working through all of this myself. Writing helps me express how I feel, even when I can't find the right words, or when nothing makes sense. The pen starts moving and my thoughts suddenly have a way to escape, with no one to tell me I'm crazy or ask why I would feel that way. No one to try and say all the right things to make me feel better. Writing lets me feel exactly how I feel in those moments, without self-criticism or the judgement of others.

I urge you to also find some way to release all those pent-up thoughts and feelings between your therapy sessions. Who you give your ear to when you are vulnerable can shape your perspective of the situation in a healthier way. It's important you release to the right people, if that is your way of expression. I've had to learn that even people who love me and want the best for me may not have the capacity to get me where I am supposed to be. Even if you don't feel ready for therapy, I encourage you to find one outlet that doesn't require anyone having to be always available. Otherwise, you will feel frustrated and overwhelmed when you are in those situations and don't have access to that person. Again, I'm still working through this one, and being more intentional about it as well.

Eleven
Self-Development

Let's talk Self-development. A word I feel no one likes, at least at first. It puts 100% responsibility on YOU, because no one can do it for you. You have to want it for it to work and be willing to put in the effort, whatever it takes.

Don't rob yourself any longer! It takes discipline and a lot of sacrifice to heal and to grow, but it wasn't until I started working on me that I started figuring out who I really was. What I needed, what I didn't need, what helped, and what didn't. Staying in one spot - no matter how shaky - feels safer than moving forward, but that's where you can wither and die inside. Self-development is a decision you have to make, regardless of how you feel, but you have to love yourself enough to do it anyways.

You may literally find yourself having a whole argument with yourself to do something that will benefit you in the long run, rather than doing something that makes you feel less fearful in the moment.

So what am I referring to when I say Self-development? That depends on where you are in your current state of pain or growth. What are some realistic ways you feel would develop and help you grow mentally, emotionally, physically and spiritually? Therapy can help you mentally and emotionally, and may even help you spiritual as well, depending on the therapist or the outlet you choose. As you saw, some on my journal entries were prayers to God. One way for me that I've seen growth making daily decisions to be better each day than yesterday. A lot of people get tripped up when setting goals by putting hard numbers on things, like weight loss, bank accounts, or whatever it is you are pursuing. But when those numbers are not reached in the time they wanted, or they're not seeing the results they wanted, that's when discouragement can cause people to give up. The results come regardless, but we have a tendency of setting unrealistic goals. It's just a set cycle of being in the exact same place the next go round. I've also realized if we put caps on things, we can unknowingly put a number that God wanted to double, expecting Him to work according to our deadlines. And once we reached what we thought was our goal, we quit trying as hard. We stop pursuing it with the same passion. So, fall in love with just being better every day, and making decisions that will help you grow in all areas of your life.

If your goal is to be healed and forgive, Netflix ain't going to do it for you. Neither will continuing to talk about it to your friends.

If your health is a priority, quit buying the snack cakes and get a gym membership.

If you'd like to break poverty off your family and quit living paycheck to paycheck, then quit buying unnecessary items. You might also have to say no to some invites that cost money. It's a sacrifice you make for your future and where you want to be.

You do the natural and God will do the super.

You have a part to play in the process. I'm just trying to be real with you because I want you to have victory in all areas of your life. I want you to live the life God intended for you to have.

I had to learn the hard way. You have to be intentional. I'm nowhere near the finish line but I'm also nowhere near the starting line. I'm in the race, right there with you.

For the first time, I feel I'm operating in a spiritual relationship, rather than just trying to check something off a checklist for that day. I saw the typical 'church life' modeled, where we went to church every Sunday and occasional Wednesday, but never did anything on my own outside of that. No fundamentals.

Unfortunately, I trained myself to be a lazy Christian. Going to get what I needed on Sunday, and then barely come crawling back the next Sunday, because I did not apply any of it to my life throughout the week. Not much fruit was produced. I got good at following the rules with not much real relationship.

I've once heard that immature Christians have to stay in crisis to stay committed. That God would elevate you, but then lose you because we have a tendency to only stay committed when things are falling apart. Only pray when we are going through something.

Ouch, that hurt!

I am also one that struggles with reading and understanding the word. I was an eighth-grade dropout that never did much studying. It doesn't come natural for me. I have found my main substance for reading the word is the Bible app. I stay consistent in my devotionals pretty much daily and make sure I am at least putting something in.

Do what makes you feel comfortable and go at your own pace but just make sure you are doing something. I can't tell you how many times I have been fought by the enemy because I didn't know the word or couldn't pray like so and so. I've just come to a place, thank God, that I accept where I am. As long as I know I am actively in pursuit, I'm in the race. Growth will come with consistency. I just have to stick with it. But one area that I do feel has played a huge role in my mindset changing is watching sermons or motivation speeches on my own throughout the week. I sometimes start one on Monday and don't even get through the whole thing until Thursday or Friday. My guy, Michael Todd be going in for two hours on a Sunday, but I'm all for it! It's packed full of knowledge and revelation! I watch a couple of times a week, thirty to forty minutes each night. I take a lot of notes, and it has shifted how I think and operate. I can see the change in my perspective on circumstances that hit home. I have noticed when "life" hits, because it always will, I am not caught so off-guard. I am more stable in my emotions and what I let my mind entertain. I find myself responding rather than reacting.

Again, your own pace, your own schedule.

Whatever you fill yourself with will come out in moments that you don't expect. I got sick of toxic behavior flowing out when I was caught off-guard. That's not saying I have mastered this yet, so please don't get it twisted. My point is you have to be intentional on development. You have to commit to growing. Don't get comfortable with just mediocre when you are built for greatness!! You have to see it in yourself and want to pull it out!

When I discovered a pastor that I could receive from, nine times out of ten his sermon series were related to an area of my life that I was struggling with at the time. I immediately saw such a mindset change. For example, after I left my marriage and moved in with my brother for a few weeks, I remember looking around on the internet for something to watch. Churches were still in a weird place because of Covid, and I didn't really have a "home church" back then. I tuned into Transformation Church from time to time and remembered I liked the pastor's style of preaching, so I searched him on YouTube. Wouldn't you know it, because God is funny like that, they were just starting a series called "FU"

At first, I was like, you know, that's right. But soon I learned it stood for Forgiveness University. I laughed for real, like out loud. I was like, "Dang God! You can't just give me a minute? Maybe have a series on the brokenhearted and let me just feel that for a while?" But, nah, we ain't doing it that way again. He was like, "Let's get to business. We ain't got the time to sit here in all that. It's time to GROW UP!"

I discovered through that series that I had to forgive myself first. You thought I was gonna say forgive my ex-husband, didn't you? But it had to start with me, forgiving myself for my part in all of it. Owning up to my own failures and fears. I ain't gonna lie and say that was easy to come to terms with. It's always easier pointing the finger and playing the victim, but that did nothing but hold me hostage to the assault on my heart that was connected to it. That whole sermon series was so on time. It helped me walk right through my trauma and not hiding within it anymore. It helped me realize that every pain was a lesson and learning from my circumstances would help me to never be trapped in them again. I knew I suffered, but I discovered that I didn't suffer well, picking up a lot of ugly characteristics from what I had gone through. But the biggest lesson of all was that all that pain, all the suffering, all that victimization didn't have to be my story moving forward.

I want to share an entry from that series. I was separated and moving towards divorce for the second time.

November 29, 2020

Well, here I sit. In a whirlwind of emotions! I can't really pinpoint exactly how to describe how I'm feeling. Sad, mad, heavy, light, etc.. It's like I have all the right feelings but still have some roots of the bad ones. I know that's just an indicator that something needs attention. So I'm going to try and express it! Like I'm happy and grateful for the growth I've seen in me lately. I'm happy and feel so much love from family and friends - support is needed this time. But then if I let myself sit long enough, I feel sad, because a part of me misses him and wishes things could have been different. I'm pissed that he's hurt me so much and so deeply. I'm pissed that our story ended but also hopeful for the future God has for me because I know this ain't it! I get discouraged in moments, like scared that there's nothing better. That I will never feel again. I will never trust again. But I shouldn't have to make God convince me of His promises. His word don't lie! I'm still adjusting to my new norms and getting used to the boundaries that are in place. I understand their need, but it's still hard!

At times I feel so broken, so hurt like I hate what I've been through and it still knocks me down at times. Gets to the deep parts within. I've struggled my whole life with wondering how and why people hurt me, leave me, how they don't protect me or love me enough. But I realize hurt people hurt people, but what's that say about me? I'm hurt but don't want to hurt people. Well, I do but I don't! I'm sad, like for real. My heart is broken and feels so much pain and sadness. I can feel a sense of numbness trying to attach itself, because I can't or haven't been able to 'feel' things I normally would. I gotta get to the root of that because it's scary.

I can hear so much strength in that journal entry, despite the confusion and the acceptance of reality of the circumstance. I can hear frustration, but I can also hear hope. I love how it ends, and even for me now, it shows me GROWTH. It ends by saying

"I gotta get to the root because it's scary!" What does that express? My responsibility? Work that I have to do? No one can dig up that root for me or go back though my pain and hurt. No one can deal and process it. It doesn't matter if it's gonna take me weeks or years, I'm gonna dig it up! You have to get to a place you want better, a place you know that there's so much more for you! God will do his part, if you will commit to doing yours.

When you get intentional on development, and you get desperate for growth, you have to put in the work. Period. It doesn't just happen. If I wanted to stay where I was, mentally and emotionally, I would probably would have found myself repeating a cycle. You can't walk into something new if you're scared to walk out of something old! God wants seasons, not cycles. For my mental and emotional health, I seemed to always be looking for ways to not get stuck. I say stuck, because of thought patterns that would try to sneak back in. Triggers that would serve a notice, and just new situations I found myself in for the first time had me always looking for ways to assist myself.

That's why I have said YOU HAVE to figure out what works for you. I remember there was a really low time emotionally that I hit a few months back. I was encouraged by my mentor to check out one of Mel Robbins' videos.

I quickly became a fan of hers and loved how she was so relatable and realistic about things that we may tend to struggle with from time to time. There was a specific video I came across that encouraged me to write 'good morning' to myself every morning, followed by one line that includes something inspirational, motivational, inspiring or affirming. One line. Nothing drastic. Like I said, I was feeling kinda down about myself, about my self-worth. I was discouraged, but when you're desperate, you will do anything, even at the risk it will fail. But it didn't. Here's a week or so of those affirmations, just to give you an example.

November 10, 2020

Good morning, Britt! You are worth more. No one is worth sacrificing your peace for!

November 16, 2020

GM, Queen! Rock out today! Remember you are amazing!

November 18, 2020

GM, wonderful woman! You may feel a void this morning, an emptiness, but that will not last forever. Keep your mind right and focused on things that are true!

November 19, 2020

GM, Britt. Remember whose you are. You are loved. Love yourself back!

November 20, 2020

GM, Queen. Never lower your vibration again or stoop down to a lower level. Keep your head up! Love you today!

November 21, 2020

GM, Britt. Love you, and love others!

It, for real, tears me up re-reading those, because I remember where I was and the strength it took to write things to me when I felt the complete opposite at that time. But realistic ways that fit your life and your schedule have a positive impact on your mental health. They are so vital. Again, you only get out of things what you are willing to put in.

I remember at first feeling awkward writing those, because you have to really apply yourself when affirming something you don't necessarily feel. Then I saw how just speaking positively to myself started to encourage me. Doing that each day remind me of who I am and what I had to offer! When you start to prioritize yourself, to see and appreciate yourself for everything you are, you will start to take better care of you.

The first relationship, outside of God, is the one with YOU!

Do the work, LOVE YOU.

Twelve

Finding Your Vision

Once again, I need to express how important it is to have someone in your corner pushing you to become a better version of yourself and encouraging you to stretch out of your comfort zone. The ones that refuse to let you quit. The ones that know you are so much more than what you are going through! Could be a relative or a friend, but now that I am writing, I see how important that role was to me throughout this process and still is.

I was encouraged by my mentor to create a vision board. In the beginning, he was on speed dial, and I called him up at every hiccup or bump in the road and he made himself available to me. But I will also say there came a time that I was encouraged to walk, instead of crawl. What I mean by that is, he took the training wheels off of our relationship. He had a hard conversation with me, that at first, I could have picked up offense from. I could have taken it personally, but I saw it for what it really was - an expression of love. No one had ever told me, "Okay, Brittany. You are stronger than you are giving yourself credit for. It's time to get started doing things on your own and not relying on me so much.

I've had many relationships in the past that I could call anytime I was faced with adversity, or whenever I felt I needed safety, or help to make a decision. I would call them first, before I even responded, reacted or even prayed. I let these people play deciding roles in my life, because I never really trusted myself and didn't want the pressure of having to make a tough decision. I just couldn't stand to blame myself, if things didn't work out the way they were supposed to. And some people honestly take pride in being the one you call in every crisis and look for opportunities to come in and save the day. You can love those heroes in your life, but there's no growth for you as an individual if you keep doing that. With my mentor's words I experienced tough love for the first time!

Here's the entry that I made after that conversation.

November 30, 2020

So tonight, I realized something. Something that I already knew I struggled with, but never had someone care enough about me to call it out. I rely on people way too much, for happiness, for help and some people feed on that. The feeling of feeling needed. But I need to learn how to walk on my own! I gotta stop crawling and start walking then running on my own two feet! I gotta get my fundamentals on my own, and realize that when things start going bad, it's time to press into Him and not other people!

I want to be strong enough to withstand trails and struggles without having to run to someone! Because what if that person is unavailable, on vacation, going through something themselves? Then, what?

I gotta do this.

I will do this.

I have to do this!

I want to be free from the need to always feel like I have to have someone! It's self-sabotaging honestly. To fully rely on someone is a set-up. People fail. They don't meet expectations all the time, and that's okay! That's why we shouldn't put our trust in people, only in God.

I gotta refocus. I have been feeling discouraged, lost a little hope, and been sad about my present reality. All these things are okay to feel, but not okay to be!

Feelings are indicators of an area that needs some tending to,. Healing and encouragement are not reasons to get depressed and stuck! I have the tools and resources. I just have to apply them! Use them! Then pass them on to someone else!

It took some adjusting for sure, but I can finally say here I am because of it. I'm thankful for the people God has surrounded me with. My mentor and I still meet regularly to this day, about once or twice a month, and it's scheduled. No more two or three random phone calls a day. I honestly don't know how he dealt with me for those first few months, it must have been exhausting! Our relationship is stronger for it.

Coach… if you are reading this, and I know you will be, I want you to know how extremely grateful I am for all the times you stopped what you were doing to make yourself available to me. Thank you for your prayers and encouragement, and most of all, for your push! The assignments that you would strategically give me, or just being an ear when I needed someone to listen, helped me not feel not so alone in the middle of all that chaos. I felt cared for, loved. From the moment you came to my brother's house to make sure that everyone in my circle was onboard with holding me accountable to my boundaries and helping me adjust to what my new normals would be, I sat there and realized I had a team. One that wasn't unknowingly biased to a side but one that was for what was best, regardless. Thank you for seeing something in me that I had never seen in myself. And thank you so much for never letting me quit. That was such a pivotal time in my life, and I thank

God for your obedience. I appreciate you more than words could express. Thank you, Coach. You have helped me become the woman I am today.

Like I said, everyone needs extra support, and maybe even a push in the beginning. My mentor did that for me, but again there comes a time when you have to level up and take responsibility for your own life. He was obedient to God, and I'm sure that conversation was hard for him to give, as much as it was for me to receive. But I can't stress this enough.... No one can do it for you. You have to want it bad enough that you refuse to make excuses or let how you feel dictate your actions.

My mentor had encouraged me to create a vision board. This was frustrating and overwhelming every time I thought about starting. I didn't even know myself at that moment, let alone what I wanted in the future. It was hard to dig deep into hope and consider visions. Visions for me, my family, career, hobbies, financial, health, etc. But he reminded me that I needed to write it down to make it clear! So I was willing to give it a shot, and this is what I came up with.

December 10, 2020

Vision statement about me:

Looking ahead to the future, where do I see myself? Emotionally, mentally, financially, career-wise, family, living quarters, etc... There is so much to factor in when considering this. Well, here it goes...

Emotionally - Secure, confident in my decisions and in myself, not easily triggered by trauma, a different perspective on what I've been through. Self-development.

Mentally - healthy thoughts, more affirmations, more self-love, confidence, discipline.

Financially - debt free, having financial freedom, tithe regularly, bless others, savings.

Career - take on more responsibility, lead position, take value and find purpose in what I'm doing, work unto God, get my associates degree.

Family - love again, trust again, have stability in my home, love hard with my kids

Home - would like to stay in Bullitt County but get a newer house. Nothing crazy big at all small and homey, but desire something newer.

So, to sum up the key points into a vision statement…

DON'T LOSE HOPE!

Hope is the only thing that gives tomorrow a chance to be different from today. I started small and just thought about the things I wanted for myself and my family. I went out and got a poster board, printed off some images from the internet, got some markers and just went at it.

I still have that vision board hanging on my wall, so I can see it every morning when I roll out of the bed. I look at it and remind myself of where I want to be, where I want to go. If I can take one or two steps in any of those areas in a day, that's a win for me. Even if there's a day I miss the mark, I try again the next day. You just can't give up! Creating a vision board will be something I do consistently. I'm still learning to have grace for myself. My whole life is different now. I am trying to figure out my identity, while adjusting to my new normal; growing, healing, unlearning survival tactics that have attached to my personality, being a single mom, and so much more.

Something I recently heard was…

What if it's not about becoming anything at all, but unbecoming everything you're not, so that you can be exactly who you were meant to be in the first place?

That really is a lot, and I have to be patient in the process. Healing takes time, but I refuse to quit because I see myself so differently now. I can actually say I love this woman that I am becoming. I see her for the first time as an individual, as a real person. Not just a mother or a wife, or any other role she has to play, but as an individual who deserves better from me. She's more than just what she can do for everyone else. She has her own needs and is strong enough to do it for herself.

So please, prioritize you. Love you first. From there you will be able to properly love others and to receive the love you've always deserved. But it has to start with you!

Physical growth/health... Now this is a topic I love. I love walking into the gym, AirPods in and a fire playlist ready to push me to my limits. When I go to the gym, I don't think. Like for real, it's wild. I guess you could say it's an escape, but that sounds like a crutch, when it's not. It's an hour and a half of just *being*. Not thinking of where I am, mentally or emotionally. Not thinking of what I've been through or am going through. Not figuring out my to-do list of chores and responsibility. It's just being in that very moment.

If you are anything like me, getting a break from being in my own head was like a five-star vacation. I would consider myself a Stage 5 over-thinker. I have a tendency to think of every possible scenario when faced with certain decisions, or replay those situations in my mind, over and over again. It was so empowering to have a minute where I was out of my head and loving myself in action, making my health a priority. The results of exercise and good health also help your mental and emotional states, because when you look good, you feel good! It's a win-win!

By working out, I've learned that consistency and discipline are better than anything else. If you can get disciplined and consistent with exercise, it rolls over into all other areas of your life. When you create a habit of not letting feelings sap your strength, when you push past the "I don't feel like it" days, when excuses are recognized for what they are, and not be seen as insurmountable problems, then you begin to understand how powerful you really are inside. You may not feel like it but you do it anyway, which then trains you to not let feelings, fears and negative thoughts rule your life. You learn to fight against those thoughts and feelings that don't align with your future and just do what you need to, REGARDLESS of how you feel! You just have to show up. Your life changes when your mind changes. He states in Romans that you are transformed by the renewing of your mind, and *HE MEANT THAT!*

There were some days I was only able to work out for thirty minutes due to a busy schedule or my mood that day, but I did SOMETHING!

Just don't quit!

There were weeks I was reminded I was a human and not a robot, so I would miss three days in a row, because of life just being busy with working OT, kids sports, etc. But even then, I jumped back on as soon as I could.

Your main focus has to be to stay focused.

Thirteen
Taking the Leap

Keep reminding yourself why you need to make the effort to Self-improve, and then love yourself enough to actually do it! For some it may be for health reasons. Even if you do not need to lose weight, working out is still good for your health. For me, it was one-hundred percent mental. I knew if I missed a day or two, I'd feel it. I'd lose focus, I had to show up for myself so many times, when I didn't want to. What that does over time is build trust within yourself. You are proving that you can get things done. That you can keep your commitments. And I started realizing I could rely on myself! When we make promises and then don't come through, we subconsciously let ourselves down. This, in turn, creates a negative outlook and wounded esteem towards ourselves!

The one person you should always be able to count on is you! If you say you are going to work out, do it! If you say you are gonna get up early and read something constructive before you start your day, do it!

Whatever it is, start giving yourself the love you give others! If your spouse, sibling, or friend told you that they were going to pick you up and take you somewhere, but then ten minutes before they were supposed to be there, they called and canceled, saying "they no longer felt like it." How would that make you feel? Imagine it for real. That's how you are making yourself feel every time you make a promise to yourself and then don't come through. It may not feel bad at the moment, but over time it creates a negative outlook on how you see yourself!

If you can't imagine doing that to anyone else you love, then why do it to yourself? How many times have you told yourself you were gonna be there and didn't show up, this year alone?

Here is an entry in my Self-Care Journal:

November 28, 2020

The journey... The process... Sheesh! Anyone who has truly walked out either or both of those terms knows they are a beast! It's not for the faint of heart or quitters! Salute to the ones that are with me on finding self, healing, purpose and identity! It comes with higher highs and lower lows, but one thing for certain, I have not been alone for one second! As life has changed, I'm reminded that God remained the same. It's okay to acknowledge where you are, as long as you know it's not where you are staying. I refuse to get paralyzed by what I've been through. The assault on my past, yes, has wounded my soul, but I refuse to let it cause uncertainty for the future. I will never make God have to convince me of His promises again! Hope is my anchor, and I'm throwing it into the future because I refuse to drown in the past!

What it took me all this time to learn is that I still have so much left to learn. I will never be where I feel I am done, at my peak, the end. That's just my mindset though. Seeing and discovering all that I am capable of so far has made me realize there's so much more to me than I ever imagined. Growth doesn't come easy, that's for sure, but does anything worth having? I refuse to settle for anything less than what I I deserve. I say that even while still wrestling with what exactly I feel I deserve. I know I deserve forgiveness, as do all God's children. I know I deserve to be happy. So, right now, I am going to do whatever I can to achieve that. To make myself happy! But happiness doesn't always fall from the sky, it can only be found with action. Yeah, that 'actions speak louder than words' quote is true. I can talk all day about how I am going to do something, but until I actually make myself get up and do it, it's nothing but empty promises! Same with faith. Without work faith withers away, which implies there's a side to it that is your responsibility.

I am still working through my insecurities and the healing I have yet to do, but trust that whatever happens in my life, good or bad, there is something to learn in it! This life takes unexpected turns, and you have to trust that God is in control. You have to refuse to revisit what you can't revive, once you have learned what you needed from it. If you don't let the pain have purpose, it hurts even more! I can sit here as I am writing and tell you I'd go through it all over again, at the risk of doing it differently and not finding out who I am becoming right now. Throughout this journey I have discovered a happiness and peace I didn't even know existed, especially alone. I've always felt I needed someone or something to make me happy, but now I know that's not true. Happiness comes from within.

Don't get me wrong, I am human and have my moments. I can feel lonely at times, but I am never really alone. Living for everyone else never allowed me to discover me, just me. To sit with myself, my decisions, my past, my doubt and my fears forced me to realize I have things in me that are broken and in desperate need of attention.

And if you are there, if you are stuck or going through something that doesn't make sense, please hear me!!

YOU are worth the fight!

GET UP!

DO it for YOU!

Yes, your kids and family are part of your *Why*, but you have to be what you need before you can be what they need!! I promise life will start to make sense again. One day at a time. Army crawl at first, if you have to, but JUST MOVE! Even if it starts as wiggling, just start moving!! I know it hurts and may seem hopeless right now but lean into God. Trust that He knows what He's doing. He just needs you to partner with Him. Do your part and He will do his! That's one thing I can promise! The more I sought Him, the more I found out about me. Who else is there to run to, other than the one who created you while you were searching for your own identity? We are created in HIS image.

A year ago, I would never have thought I'd be writing a book, sharing the story of what I've been through, BUT GOD MADE IT HAPPEN!

You can do it! I believe in you and I'm rooting for you!

Yes, you are still going to be triggered and reminded of pain. Yes, there will be hard days. That's growing pains, and all part of the process. But stop normalizing hard years or hard months and see how important that change of perspective can be. Perspective is your responsibility, and that only changes with the work you are willing to put in. No one can do that for you.

Sometimes I wish it was that way. I wish I could save all my loved ones. I wish I could just come in and do all the work for them; but that would be cheating them out of their own growth. Without the discomfort, there's nothing to learn. And if you are out to solve every problem for everyone else, you will kill yourself trying. They have their process, and you have yours. It will take discipline, sacrifice, and all the above. You need to get desperate for change, but to get over a hard past is to create an amazing future! What's in front of you is better than what is behind you.

I'm nowhere near my destination. Shoot. I'm not even convinced there is one, I'm on the same journey, same as you. One day at a time, finding purpose in each day, healing and learning to love myself and discover who I am. I am convinced that it's not about the cards you were dealt in this life, but how you play the hand.

Please don't fold!

You need YOU!

You are LOVED!

You are WORTHY!

You CAN DO IT!

The past is gone.

The future is waiting for you to make it the reality you desire.

The time to start is now.

I will pray for your success.

Dedication

To my GOD, my daughter, my son, and everyone whose played a role in my journey to healing.

First off, I have to Give All Glory to God. I wouldn't be where I am without Him! Not one part of this process could I have done without Him! He is the reason I sit here in my right mind and that I am able to share my story in confidence, knowing He has a plan for it all. There wouldn't be words to adequately describe how He has loved me through all of this. His presence has become my safe place, the place I find everything I need. The place I found me!

His love is unmatched and unwavering.

His intentionality reminds me that it's safe to have hope. His pursuit to leave the ninety-nine to come find me reminds me that I am worthy and that I have value. His presence gives me peace, and an assurance that everything is okay. His convictions remind me that He has a purpose for my life and to stay focused.

I am beyond grateful for His unconditional love. That is more than enough, nothing compares! My heart will forever cry, Hallelujah!

To my daughter, because, of course, I had to give her her own section somewhere in this book. I mean, she has asked me at least once a month if I mentioned her in my book. And of course, I did.

You are the one that made me a mother. Thank you for being exactly what I needed, when I needed it. Despite how I express that I lost my individual identity in the roles I took on at such a young age, like being a mother, does not mean for a second, I would have wanted it any other way! You give me purpose and a reason to fight as hard as I do. I want to be my best self so I can give you the life I wish I had growing up.

When I look at you, I'm reminded of my *Why's*.

Why I can't give up.

Why I can't settle for mediocre.

Why I have to hold on.

I am sorry for putting things on you that you were not ready to carry throughout this journey. Momma's still learning and trying to figure it all out.

I am sorry if I ever made you feel that anything was your fault, or if I took out my frustration on you. As I am on this journey of discovering who I am, I will make sure I come alongside you and make sure you find yourself too! I want to give you the space and guidance to become everything you are supposed to be! At the end of the day, I just want you to be happy and whole! I'm not saying every day is going to be great, or that I have all the answers, but I will do my best to be my best self for you and your brother. To give you both what I needed when I was younger, a fully healed mother.

I love you more than you will ever know and hope you never doubt it. If there is one thing I hope you know for certain, it is my love for you.

My sweet EmJay. I know at this time in your life you have so many questions when it comes to this adjustment of no longer having a two-parent household. I'm trusting as you get older, it will make more sense to you. I'm sorry I had to make a decision that hurt you now, in the hope that you won't be hurt even more in the future. But to know you is to know love. I don't think you will ever know how needed you were on some of my darkest days. You have the sweetest, tenderest little heart, and I pray that nothing in this life will cause you to lose that. When I am around you, I feel like the luckiest woman in the world. Your love is unmatched! From the million times you say 'I love you' each day to the cuddles and kisses at night. Your random acts of kindness remind me that I can receive love and affection. That I deserve it. I love you so much for that.

To everyone this past year that prayed for me, encouraged me, helped me, spent time with me, checked in with me, pushed me, loved and believed in me through it all...THANK YOU!

Special thanks to IVision Press for their partnership in helping me make this book a reality. Thank you for pushing me and believing in me throughout this process. Your encouragement is so appreciated, and I am grateful for our connection.

This is one of those 'if you know you know' paragraphs (and if you don't know, then it probably ain't about you, lol.)

I used to force myself into groups to be accepted and wanted by others. But what I came to realize was all that was rooted in my own abandonment issues, and my desire to be needed and wanted. But I have come to realize that I have to love myself first, and anything outside of that is just a bonus. I no longer seek affirmation or validation from others, but solely from God. From there, I've gained a confidence in myself that is only found in Him, because I know I am not doing this on my own. Discovering a love for myself, I don't feel as bothered when people choose to walk or pull away. Yeah, it hurts and takes some time to adjust to, but the thing with God is that, when He weeds people out, it's probably to make room for what you really need, not what you thought you needed!

He gave me a word of protection over rejection back in May, and it made so much sense! Rejection still hurts, but it helps me to see past those negative feelings. To see past the surface and look at things from a kingdom perspective.

So to those who stood beside me through all of these changes and realizations and all of those highs and lows, I thank you again for everything. The little things, like a random encouraging text at just the right time, to the phone calls, visits and all the ways you sacrificed your time, listening and investing in me. For keeping me accountable, letting me crash at your pad and stay with you while I was trying to figure out my living arrangements. From helping me with free childcare when I was adjusting to a one-income household and living paycheck-to-paycheck, to working with me so I could afford therapy sessions for both me and my daughter. For throwing one of the best surprise birthday parties of my life, even when I was at my lowest, for being intentional and staying available when I needed to know someone was there, and that someone was willing to listen with love. And for so many other things too numerous to name.

I also want to thank Pastor Michael Todd, who through his obedience changed the full trajectory of mine, especially through those seasonal messages that filled my heart, week after week.

I am sitting here today in part, because of each and every one of you! Your love, your obedience, your sacrifice, your generosity. It did not go unnoticed and is beyond appreciated.

I don't think you will ever know what it meant to me. Thank you for allowing me to make mistakes while I am trying to adjust and navigate my new normal without judgement.

Thank you for believing in me.

Thank you for seeing me, even when I didn't see myself.

And thank you for helping me find HER!

THE END

CPSIA information can be obtained
at www.ICGtesting.com
Printed in the USA
LVHW081104240822
726738LV00008B/351